CUTTING-GARDEN
QUILTS

Melinda Bula

CUTTING-GARDEN QUILTS

Fabulous Fusible Flowers

Martingale
& COMPANY

Cutting-Garden Quilts: Fabulous Fusible Flowers
© 2007 by Melinda Bula

That Patchwork Place® is an imprint
of Martingale & Company®.

Martingale & Company
20205 144th Ave. NE
Woodinville, WA 98072-8478 USA
www.martingale-pub.com

Printed in China
12 11 10 09   8 7 6 5 4

Library of Congress Cataloging-in-Publication Data
Library of Congress Control Number: 2007028425

ISBN: 978-1-56477-759-1

· **Mission Statement** ·

Dedicated to providing quality products
and service to inspire creativity.

· **Credits** ·

President & CEO ❈ *Tom Wierzbicki*
Publisher ❈ *Jane Hamada*
Editorial Director ❈ *Mary V. Green*
Managing Editor ❈ *Tina Cook*
Developmental Editor ❈ *Karen Costello Soltys*
Technical Editor ❈ *Laurie Baker*
Copy Editor ❈ *Sheila Chapman Ryan*
Design Director ❈ *Stan Green*
Assistant Design Director ❈ *Regina Girard*
Illustrator ❈ *Laurel Strand*
Cover Designer ❈ *Stan Green*
Text Designer ❈ *Regina Girard*
Photographer ❈ *Brent Kane*

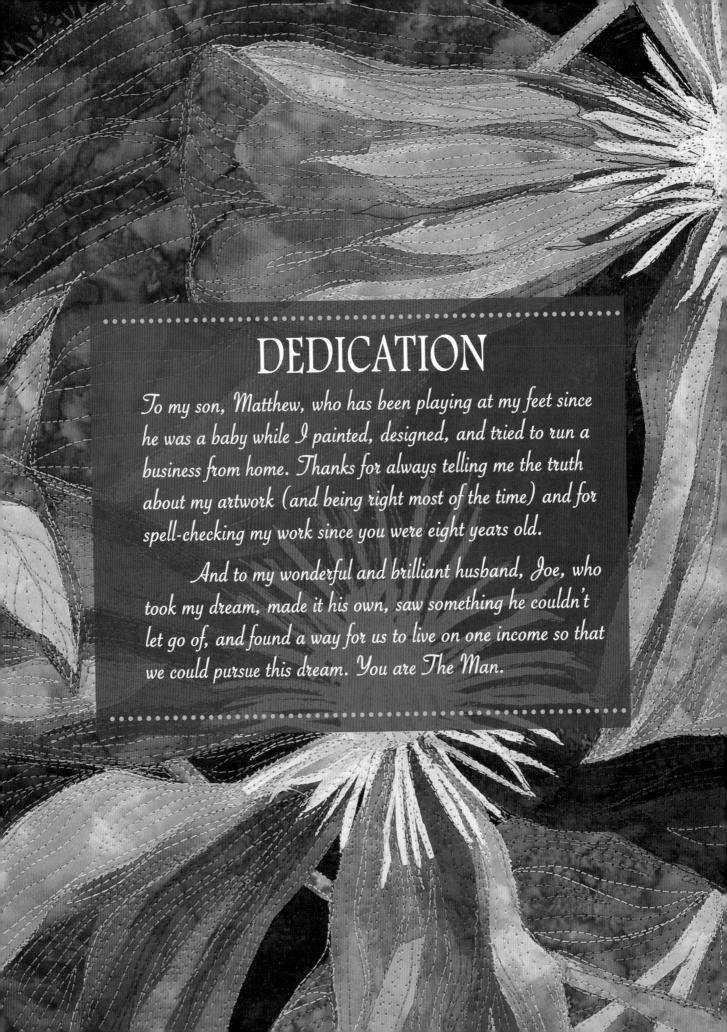

DEDICATION

To my son, Matthew, who has been playing at my feet since he was a baby while I painted, designed, and tried to run a business from home. Thanks for always telling me the truth about my artwork (and being right most of the time) and for spell-checking my work since you were eight years old.

And to my wonderful and brilliant husband, Joe, who took my dream, made it his own, saw something he couldn't let go of, and found a way for us to live on one income so that we could pursue this dream. You are The Man.

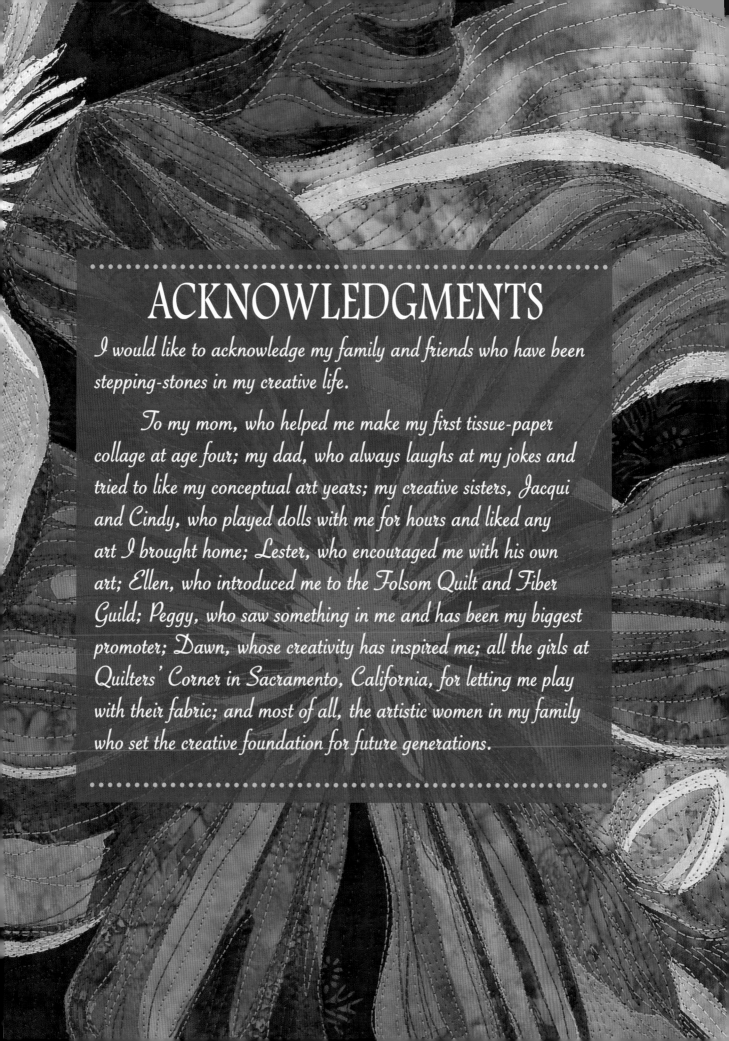

ACKNOWLEDGMENTS

I would like to acknowledge my family and friends who have been stepping-stones in my creative life.

To my mom, who helped me make my first tissue-paper collage at age four; my dad, who always laughs at my jokes and tried to like my conceptual art years; my creative sisters, Jacqui and Cindy, who played dolls with me for hours and liked any art I brought home; Lester, who encouraged me with his own art; Ellen, who introduced me to the Folsom Quilt and Fiber Guild; Peggy, who saw something in me and has been my biggest promoter; Dawn, whose creativity has inspired me; all the girls at Quilters' Corner in Sacramento, California, for letting me play with their fabric; and most of all, the artistic women in my family who set the creative foundation for future generations.

CONTENTS

INTRODUCTION

I'VE BEEN IN LOVE WITH COLOR
and fabric my entire life. Having a mother who
was an interior designer meant that color and fabric
were always part of my life. I've always wanted to
combine the two, whether it was designing fabric
and wallpaper or painting a still life on canvas.

I thought for years that I was the only one with
this mad obsession, but I'm thrilled to discover that
I'm not alone. I've found that most quilters have
this same passion. One of my first jobs as a teen was
working at a fabric store. Not any fabric store, mind
you, but a bowling alley turned into a fabric store.
When the new fabric would arrive it was just like
Christmas to me and I couldn't wait to see what we
had received. One day the owner of the store called
me into her office to ask me to please stop rubbing
my face on all the new fabrics. I had no idea I was
doing that. I think I was trying to feel color. Now
that's obsessed!

This book is about putting color and design
together. I've always loved to paint and have been
able to experience the thrill of color on canvas. But
could I create a painting using only fabric and thread?
Well, the answer is *yes!* That's how I started creating
Cutting-Garden quilts, and once again, I'm obsessed.

The world of quiltmaking has made me feel
like I belong to a wonderfully creative family with
hundreds of years of history. Not all of my quilting
sisters, past and present, think of quilting as an art
form, but to me, it always has been and always will be,
no matter how traditional or wildly artistic the final
product. I encourage you to play with your fabrics,
touch them as much as you want, and even rub them
on your face! Have fun!

HOW TO USE THIS BOOK

I WANT YOU TO EXPERIENCE the same thrill I get when I create a beautiful art quilt, and I want you to be proud enough to show off your finished creation. Everything you need to know about making Cutting-Garden quilts is included in this book, and even if you don't feel like you have an ounce of creativity in you, I assure you that anyone can make these quilts with amazing results. I have watched students of all artistic levels be successful using my technique.

I've written this book with two different learning styles in mind. For those of you who have an artistic eye and want to create your own masterpieces, the details in the next few chapters will spark your creativity and encourage you along the way. I've included ways to break down a picture, lay out the design, and most importantly, select colors. You'll find all this information and more in "Fabulous Fusible Appliqué" on page 29. After the appliqué process is complete, you'll move on to add even more details with thread painting, which is covered in "Renegade Thread Play" on page 40. Use the information in these chapters as a study guide to pursue your own creative path. You'll find that the process is a wonderful exercise for developing creativity.

For those of you who desire to make a beautiful flower quilt but don't consider yourself artistic enough to jump into your own designs, I've created five patterns that you can use like a paint-by-numbers painting—except you're using fabric instead of paint. Each of the patterns is broken down into easy-to-follow steps, and most importantly, all of the patterns include a fabric key to help you through the color-selection process. Selecting the right colors is the key to creating a great flower quilt. You'll still need to read the chapters that outline the appliqué and thread-painting techniques, but you'll find that the patterns eliminate much of the development process. Eventually, I hope you'll become comfortable enough to dabble with your own designs, but until then, I've taken care of the more challenging parts.

Before you get started, let the quilts in the "Gallery" on pages 12–25 inspire you for the creative process ahead. The quilts there will give you a feel for where I've been on my own flower-quilt journey and some of the challenges I faced along the way.

GALLERY

THE QUILTS IN THIS GALLERY are a compilation of work I've done since 2002. The earlier pieces started out simpler and the later pieces were more challenging and used more thread. Each quilt taught me a lesson and pushed my creativity as far as I thought I could go. Then, when I started working on the next quilt, I found I could go further. Each piece is like my baby. There are some tears shed in the birthing process, but what a thrill to see each one develop.

• Double Delight •
24" x 19", 2002

This was my first Cutting-Garden quilt. I wanted to see if I could use fabric like paint to capture the beauty of these roses. I soon found out that I didn't have enough colors in my stash to create the depth needed. This quilt taught me that it's not about how much fabric you have, but that you have the right fabrics.

This was my second flower quilt, and like the first, I quickly realized that I needed more depth of color in my stash—this time yellow. After a trip to the fabric store to purchase ⅛ yard of about 12 yellow fabrics, I was able to achieve the dimension needed to create the daisies. I used a brown thread and a zigzag stitch around the center of the flowers.

· Yellow Daisies ·
18" x 20", 2002

• Shasta Daisies •
26" x 38", 2002

The challenge with this wall hanging was to make white flowers that looked different but were the same. The solution was in collecting about 35 different white fabrics. I used pinkish whites, bluish whites, yellowish whites, and so on. I had to go to several shops to find all the whites I needed.

This was done as a study in green. The original picture on which I based the quilt was only 1½" square but the color was intense. However, when I enlarged the picture, I lost all the color. I had to use the original picture for color choices and the enlarged drawing for the shape of the leaves. This is my husband's favorite.

• *Clematis* •
24" x 32", 2002

Experimenting with fabrics taught me a lot. For this quilt, I wanted to see if I could use printed fabrics. I primarily use batiks, but I did throw in some subtle polka dots. The prints that worked best were all tone-on-tone fabrics. The centers of the flowers are detailed with lots of thread.

• Strawberries •
12" x 12", 2003

This quilt was created for my quilt guild's art-quilt challenge. The subject matter needed to be a fruit and the quilt could be no larger than 12" x 12". I wasn't about to cut tiny pieces of fabric for the strawberry seeds, so I used gold glass seed beads, which added a little sparkle to the quilt.

· Apple Bowl ·
38" x 45", 2003

This wall hanging won second place in the professional
division of the Sulky of America Challenge contest.
I entered hoping to win some thread, but I won a
sewing machine instead. See page 68 for instructions
on making a similar quilt.

• Oriental Poppies •
17" x 24", 2003

The paper-like petals of poppies are so delicate and the color so rich that I challenged myself to recreate the look in fabric. The poppy is a difficult flower to get right, and it took me about two months to complete this quilt. The centers of the flowers are accented with bugle beads that add a three-dimensional look to the quilt.

• Sweet Peas and Pansies •
24" x 36", 2003

Sweet peas and pansies are my favorite flowers because of their translucent quality and brilliant colors. The challenge here was to create a clear glass vase with water in it using only fabric and thread. In this close-up photo of the quilt, you can see that I met the challenge.

· Geraniums ·
36" x 36", 2004

This is the first pattern I designed for teaching the Cutting-Garden technique. The flowers were inspired by the cranesbills that grow under the roses in Monet's garden, so of course I needed them in my fabric "garden." The checked sashing and border were fused to the background fabric.

• Renaissance •
56" x 72", 2004

With a mother who was an interior designer, I was often exposed to beautiful homes and gorgeous flower arrangements. She used bouquets as the final touch to an elegant room. I would watch her as she placed each flower in just the right spot. That knowledge benefits me as I make each quilt. Stand back from your work and look at it from all sides to make sure each fabric flower is in the right spot. This quilt hangs in my living room and thrills me every day.

• Hollyhocks •
27" x 36", 2004

I sometimes have better success quilting flowers than growing them. This wall hanging was inspired by a garden filled with hollyhocks. A lot of the depth in these flowers was achieved using thread, which helped to smooth and soften the chunky pieces of fabric. Several printed fabrics were used to give depth and density to the leaves.

This is my dream bouquet; it has all of my favorite flowers in my favorite colors.
I started by selecting a black background fabric that I knew would make the flowers
stand out. Then I found a great batik that looked like marble that I used for the table.
I tucked the flowers into the vase just like I would arrange them in a real vase. This
quilt won third place in the Art-Naturescapes category and also honorable mention in the Founders
Award category at the fall 2005 International Quilt Festival, as well as honorable mention in the
Innovative category at the Pacific International Quilt Festival 2006.

· A Garden's Delight ·
45" x 62", 2005

• Social Climber Roses •
34" x 48", 2005

You can never have too many roses. When I saw this rose, called Social Climber, in a nursery, I went crazy for the color. While I was working on this quilt, I had pink fabric all over the house. My husband was doing yard work and came in the house with a handful of pink fabric scraps and thread. He had found them all over the yard. We left the colorful pile for the sparrows making their nests. The next morning the pink pile was gone. This quilt won a Judge's Choice ribbon at the Pacific International Quilt Festival 2006.

· Afternoon Glory ·
45" x 57", 2006

On a beautiful fall afternoon, the morning glories were hanging heavy with flowers over my garden fence.
Their colors had changed from blues in the morning to pinks and purples in the afternoon. I ran to get
my camera, thinking that this would make a great quilt. I captured the moment forever with this quilt.

THE CREATIVE PROCESS

CREATIVITY IS A PART of everything we do. It's in how we dress, the way we cook, and how we plant flowers in our gardens. It can even be in the way we balance our checkbook.

Creativity is a discipline. It requires practice just like any talent we want to develop, whether it is playing an instrument or designing quilts. The more you use

it, the better you get. My college art teacher, Miss Sharky, told me that Picasso got up and painted every day, whether he felt like it or not.

I'm a big believer that all of us were born with some creativity, probably more than we think. Unfortunately, many of us learned way back in kindergarten to follow the rules, to hold our crayon a certain way and, by all means, to stay inside the lines. Some of these learned behaviors have the power to stop our creative flow. Rejuvenating the flow comes when you realize that there are no wrongs when it comes to creativity. What you like is right.

Another thing that kills creativity is not believing in yourself. I love to observe my students as they work. They teach me so much. I've noticed that they all have their own way of turning on their creative flow. Some go methodically slow. Some are fast and furious, and some are in between. Each person has his

or her own personal style, and every style works. The trouble comes when we say things like "I'm not creative," "I can't do this," or "Hers is better than mine." Stop it! Erroneous beliefs like these will keep your creativity from evolving. Some of us drive slow and some of us drive fast, but we all get there eventually.

I love to analyze the creative process and have found that there are some traits and skills that are characteristic of people with a developed creative mind:

❀ They have learned that every mistake is a potential success, even if they have to start over.

❀ They let their mind and eyes look outside the box.

❀ They don't mind digging in the trash to find whatever they need to make their art perfect.

❀ They play and try new things.

❀ They realize that it's the process that counts, not the finished product.

❀ And most importantly, they persevere. That doesn't mean that they don't mess up, get mad, and have a good cry now and then. It simply means that after the crying has stopped, they go back and try again.

I was experimenting with size when I made this quilt. How large of a project could I handle under my sewing machine? The only way to know was to make a large quilt and see.

· Group of Pansies ·
56" x 56", 2004

A PLACE TO WORK

AS A QUILTER, YOU NEED A PLACE to call your own, somewhere you can leave out a project while you're working on it. Having your own space allows you to work whenever you get a few minutes, without having to get things ready every time. You can just pick up where you left off.

Your designated work space doesn't have to be big, it just needs to be workable, organized, and clean. I'm not super neat but I like to be somewhat organized. Nothing can deplete the creative flow faster than having to stop and dig through a pile of stuff to find something you need. Designate a place for everything, and then make sure you put items back in their places when you're finished using them. By doing this you'll be able to stay organized even in the middle of a big project.

Making Cutting-Garden quilts will be messy. Soon your room will be filled with flying fabrics and colorful threads. Little bits and pieces of fabric will be everywhere, including the seat of your pants and the bottom of your shoes. (You may want to check yourself before going off to the grocery store.) It's hard to keep the room clean in the midst of a project, but I find that cleaning up after my last project helps me get ready for the next one.

One of the best and most useful tools I have is my new studio, which also doubles as a guest bedroom. My husband, Joe, built it for my 50th birthday. With plenty of storage and two large design walls, it's 600 square feet of artistic heaven. Before I had my new space, I had worked for years in a small room off of the master bedroom. The room was not only small, but also gave my husband a direct view of my creative space (translate that to messy den) from his side of the bed, so Joe has benefited from the new studio as well.

Like most quilters, I work on more than one project at a time. I have two design walls, one on each side of the doorway, that allow me the space to do that. They are made of sound board and covered in flannel. Sound board is a lightweight, low-density porous sheet, usually ½" thick and measuring 4' by 8'. It's available at home-improvement centers, frequently where drywall is stocked, and is primarily used as a sound-deadening material. It is ideal for a design wall because it is easy to install and is gentle on your fingers when pinning your design to it. Behind the design walls is a storage area for my fabric, quilts, and wearable art. I also hide my ironing board there.

My cutting table is 6' x 4' and just the right height. It has 15 drawers on each side. My room also has two sewing stations, one for traditional quilting and the other for making Cutting-Garden quilts. My sewing tables also can be raised to cutting-table height, which is helpful when basting a large quilt. Lots of lighting over each station is a must.

Another must in my sewing room is an idea board. Everyone needs an idea board to display favorite things and ideas that inspire you. When your ideas get put in a drawer, they tend to get forgotten. Keep them visible.

THIS SECTION WILL COVER the first part of the Cutting-Garden process. Details for everything from choosing your subject matter to making the patterns to appliquéing the pieces in place are included here.

Gather Your Supplies...................

This is a list of the supplies you will need for the appliqué portion of the Cutting-Garden quilts process. Additional supplies will be required to add the thread detailing, which is done after the fabric-fusing process is complete; these supplies will be covered in "Renegade Thread Play" on page 40. If you don't already own the supplies listed, you should be able to find them at your local quilt shop.

Steam-A-Seam 2. This is your most important supply. I like Steam-A-Seam 2 because it is a double-stick, pressure-sensitive fusible web, which means it's sticky on both sides. This allows you to temporarily position an appliqué to your background fabric. Because the adhesive is temporary until you fuse it in place, you can change the appliqué placement until you're satisfied. This works much better than using pins because the appliqués lie flush against the quilt top, just like they will in the finished piece.

Steam-A-Seam 2 comes in different widths and is available in packages and by the yard. I like the 18" width because it fits perfectly on a fat quarter. Be sure you choose regular Steam-A-Seam 2 and not Lite Steam-A-Seam, which I find does not stick as well.

Iron and ironing board. I use a regular household iron with a steam feature. Because you will be working with fusible web, I advise either covering your ironing board with a piece of muslin before you begin working or covering your work with a press cloth. If fusible web adheres to your iron, heat it to the highest setting and then wipe off the webbing with a thick towel. I've also found that rubbing a hot iron over a fabric-softener sheet will remove the fusible web—and it leaves a nice smell in your house.

Sharpie marker. You will need an ultra-fine-point black Sharpie marker for several steps in the process.

Glass-head pins. Sometimes the fusible web doesn't stick as much as you need and you may need to pin the appliqués in place here and there. Glass-head pins won't melt if you iron over or near them.

A steam iron and double-sided fusible web are the mainstays of Cutting-Garden quilts.

Scissors for paper and fabric. You should have a pair of scissors that is used exclusively for cutting paper and fusible web and another pair that is used only to cut fabric. Be sure your scissors are sharp so that you get nice clean cuts. Sometimes the scissors get a little bit sticky from the fusible web, so if that bothers you, you may want to get a pair just for making Cutting-Garden quilts. However, the fusible web can be washed off with warm soapy water.

Teflon pressing sheet. This is another helpful tool for keeping the fusible-web material off your ironing board. It also lets you fuse all the parts of a flower together right on the sheet and then peel the whole unit off so you can adhere it to your quilt as a whole rather than fusing each individual piece to your quilt.

Tracing paper and freezer paper. Tracing paper is needed to make an outline drawing from the picture of your flower. For most projects, 9" x 12" sheets work fine, but larger sheets are also available. You can find tracing paper at most office- and art-supply stores. After the outline drawing is enlarged you will use freezer paper to make your patterns.

Other types of paper, such as white drawing paper or butcher paper, also can be used, but most quilters have freezer paper on hand. Whatever you choose, be sure you can see through it to transfer the drawing.

Rotary ruler and cutter. These tools are needed to square up the appliquéd quilt top.

Design board. It's really important to have a design wall or design board. Most finished quilting projects will be viewed flat on a table or bed, but a Cutting-Garden quilt will hang on a wall. You need to lay out the pieces using that perspective as well. The vertical view helps you see if the colors and shapes are balanced and working, much like a painter uses an easel.

You can easily make a design board out of foam-core board, available at office-supply and craft stores. The design board should be as large as the quilt. Duct tape more than one board together if necessary to achieve the correct size. If you want, the board can be covered with flannel to make it useful when laying out quilts other than Cutting-Garden quilts.

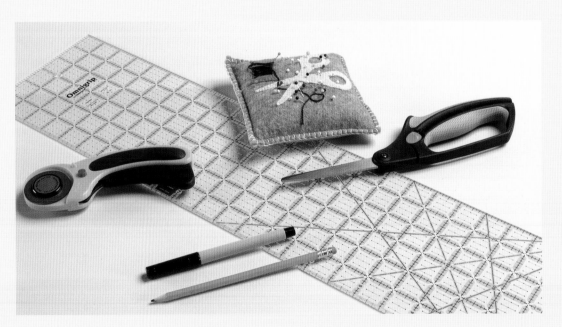

Before beginning your project, assemble cutting, marking, measuring, and pinning tools.

Find the Subject Matter ....

All of my quilts start with a picture. Because flowers are the subject of my quilts, I find that home-and-garden magazines or flower catalogs are a good place to begin.

The size of the picture is not important. I've used pictures as small as 1½" square as an inspiration because the colors thrilled me. My "Hops" quilt on page 15 is an example of this. I enlarged the original picture so that I could see the leaf shapes more clearly, but I used the 1½" square original for all my color choices.

Lately I've been taking more and more photos of flowers that would make great quilts. With a digital camera (I recommend one that has at least 5.1 megapixels) and my computer and printer, I can crop or enlarge the photo, intensify the color, and do other editing functions until I have just the right picture— all from my home. Then I print it out and am ready to start on my quilt.

I'm always looking for inspiration wherever I go—in my garden, at the beach, and on trips. I've even made my own flower arrangements and photographed them, which has also given me quite a collection of vases. Take your camera with you the next time you go out, especially if you're going to the nursery or garden center, and start your collection of inspiring photographs.

I took this photo at the garden center.

Once you've found or taken the picture that you want to transform into a quilt, you need to analyze it and make sure you love it, either for the flower itself or the colors. Hopefully it's both. The important thing is that you are thrilled by this picture. You will be staring at it for a long time, so it should be something that excites you. I find that I can persevere through the tough parts in the creative process if I really love my picture and subject matter. It's a shame to work on something that you really don't like or something you feel you have to do.

To be sure you've selected the right picture, answer the following questions:

1. What first attracted you to the picture?

2. Do you like the subject matter?

3. Do you love the color?

If you answered, "It goes with Aunt Ruby's sofa," or "I need to use up some of my stash" to any of those questions, you may want to reconsider your choice. Making a Cutting-Garden quilt needs to include some amount of fun and satisfaction for you, even if you are giving it to Aunt Ruby.

*It's fun to look through a pile of magazines
and get inspired to make something beautiful.*

Make an Outline Drawing ....

Now that you've selected your picture, you need to make an outline drawing of the parts you want to include in the quilt. The outline drawing will help you isolate the colors in the picture and the shapes those colors take, and ultimately it will be used to make the pattern pieces for each of those color shapes. Follow all the steps if you are working from your own picture. If you are using the patterns in this book, I have taken care of everything but enlarging the pattern.

• Copying Your Picture •

The first thing you need to do is make some copies so that you can analyze the shapes within the picture. Take your picture to the copy center or use your home computer and color printer. (This is where having a technology-savvy teenager around can really help.)

1. Enlarge the picture to fit an 8½" x 11" sheet of paper.

2. Make two color copies of the enlarged picture. You will use one for making the outline drawing; the other will be used for reference. Make these color copies on regular white printer paper. It is easier to draw on than glossy paper.

3. Keep the original picture to use as a color reference when choosing your fabrics. Even with the best color copiers, enlarging and copying the picture reduces the intensity of the colors. And as I said before, color is an important part of the process!

• Defining the Color Shapes •

1. Using an ultra-fine-point Sharpie marker, outline the shape of the flowers directly on one of the color copies. You do not have to include every flower and bud, only the ones you want in your quilt.

2. Draw around the center shape of each flower.

3. Outline the color shapes in each flower. A color shape is where you see the color changing in value. Sometimes it helps if you squint, or if you wear glasses, take them off. If you think you see a color change, you probably do. Outline it.

4. Mark the leaves and any other shapes you want to include in the same manner.

Prepare the color copy for tracing.

Can you see the color differences between the original picture (front) and the enlarged copy (back)?

5. Lay a piece of tracing paper over the outlined color copy and transfer all of the drawn lines to the tracing paper with your ultra-fine-point marker. When you remove the paper, you will have an outline drawing that is ready to be enlarged.

Transfer the markings to tracing paper.

*The finished outline drawing shows
all of the color shapes.*

• Enlarging the Outline Drawing •

The next step is to enlarge the black-and-white outline drawing to the desired size. If your drawing is approximately 8" x 10" and you want a quilt that finishes to approximately 24" x 30", enlarge your drawing 300%. If that seems too large, try a smaller percentage. Remember, you will need to get whatever size you've chosen onto the bed of your sewing machine later when you do the thread embellishment.

There are several ways to enlarge your drawing. In today's world of home computers and scanners, we have a wealth of tools at our disposal. The problem is the time it takes to learn all the new techniques. I like to keep it as simple as possible for my students and myself and prefer the ease and convenience of a copy shop. Any shop that makes blueprint enlargements will be able to enlarge your drawing in one piece. A regular home photocopy machine can also enlarge your drawing, but you will have to enlarge it in sections and then tape the pieces together. You can also use a desktop scanner, graph paper, or an overhead projector to make your enlargement.

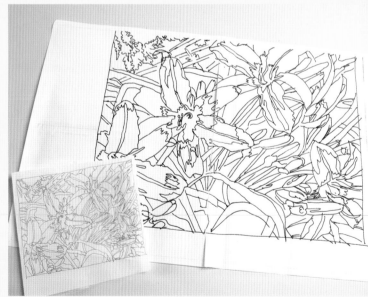

*I enlarged the traced drawing on my home computer.
It printed on several pieces of paper that I taped together.*

Create a Color Palette ....

Creating a color palette that works is what makes a Cutting-Garden quilt great. The more colors the better. A painter squeezes paint out onto a palette and mixes all the colors he needs. We are painting with fabric, so you will need to start by collecting all the colors of fabric you need.

Your color palette needs to include tints and shades of color, as well as different color values. Don't worry if you're not familiar with these terms; I'm going to explain them here. Plus, if you choose to make any of the projects in this book, each one includes a fabric key that acts as a color chart to help you along the way.

• *Exploring Color Terms* •

Color is a subject on which entire books have been written. While it is helpful to know as much as you can about the subject, your picture is going to do most of the work for you. However, I want to familiarize you with a few basic color concepts so you will be more aware of them in your picture and understand how they can work for you.

Value. Value is the lightness or darkness of a color. Your color palette needs to include a variety of light, medium, and dark fabrics to make your flowers and leaves look real and add dimension. Let's use the leaves in the picture at left as an example. If you look closely, you'll see every value from a very light yellowish green to an almost-black green. If you only used one value of green, even if they were different fabrics, the background would appear flat and unappealing.

Value is also relative to other colors around it. The blue fabrics in the photo at right are arranged with the dark values at the top, the medium values in the middle, and the light values on the bottom. However, if you were to take the lightest fabric at the bottom and a medium fabric from the middle, the medium would be considered a dark value compared to the lighter fabric. In the same manner, a medium-value fabric from the center of the group placed next to a dark-value fabric could then be considered a light value in relation to the darker fabric.

Tint. When you add white to a pure color it is called a *tint.* Pastels are tints. Tints are often used in Cutting-Garden quilts to depict areas where sunlight is hitting. Because they are lighter, tints will make an object look like it's closer to you. In the illustration below, the pure purple color is on the left. As you add more and more white, you create different tints of purple. If you continued to add white, you would eventually dilute the color so much that it would appear white.

Shade. Adding black to a pure color creates a *shade*. You will use shades for shadows, in the background of your quilt, and anywhere you want an object to recede. In the illustration below, the pure color is again on the left. As more and more black is added, the shade deepens.

• *Finding Just the Right Fabrics* •

It doesn't matter whether you're "shopping" through your stash or at the quilt shop, the fabric selection process is the same, although I do recommend checking what you already own first. It is an absolute must, however, to have the *original* picture of your subject matter in hand in order to make good fabric selections.

Start by analyzing your picture. Imagine it in its original three-dimensional state. What is in the background? What elements are in the foreground or most prominent? Are there elements between the background and foreground?

The first fabric you need to select is the background fabric, which will be the "canvas" onto which all your other fabrics will be fused. Analyze the picture and determine what color or colors are used in the background. It may be possible to use just one

fabric, or you may need to use several. If you're not sure what color to use, try black or a very dark green. Remember, you can change things as you go, so if you need to add another background color after you've started adding the flower elements, you'll be able to do it as long as you haven't permanently ironed the pieces in place. Just choose your background fabric(s) as best you can to start the process.

Now choose the fabrics for the remaining elements, again using the original picture as a guide. Start by identifying one color family. For example, let's say you're looking for the greens in your picture. Pull out all of the green fabrics in your stash or go to where the green fabrics are located in the fabric store. Hold your picture up to the fabrics and pull out every color that you think you see in the picture. You can use prints, but they should read as solids (read more about using prints on page 36). Start with the most obvious greens, which are usually the medium values. Pick out the light values next, and then the dark values, referring to your picture as you make your selections. Some of these might be yellowish greens or bluish greens so you might find what you're looking for in another area of your stash or the store.

Repeat this process with every color in the picture until you've found a fabric to represent each of them. Most likely you'll need to use more than one fabric source to find all the fabrics you need, so keep the original picture with you until you've found all of them; you never know when you'll have the opportunity to stop by a quilt store.

Based on the photograph, I would choose a dark green fabric for the background of this quilt.

USING PRINTS

Printed fabrics are great to include in your quilt. Sometimes they can provide added interest and surprise and often they contain just the color you need. When using prints, it is best to select fabrics that read as a solid. Batiks and subtle designs are good candidates. Large-scale prints are usually not good choices for using as large pieces. However, if you look carefully, you might find just the right color in a highlight or shadow of the print. In that case, just cut out the part that you need. Remember, nothing is final until it's fused in place, so you can always try it and if it doesn't work, throw it back in your stash.

These fabrics are beautiful, but the prints are too large for a Cutting-Garden quilt.

Prints that read as solids are your best choice.

• Purchasing Yardage •

If you're making a project from this book, the fabric keys include yardage amounts. For other projects, the amount of fabric you buy depends on the project and your personal wants and needs.

The background fabric is the easiest to calculate. Purchase a piece that is no smaller than the size of your enlarged drawing. If you will be using more than one fabric for the background, be sure each piece of fabric is large enough to cover the intended area of the background.

Exact yardage amounts are more difficult to determine for the remaining fabrics, although you can generally be sure you won't need more than what you purchased for the background. In my beginning quilting years, when I was on a fabric budget, I learned to make every scrap count—a fat quarter generally worked because I had to make it work. Now I find that a half-yard cut seems to work better and gives me more leeway to play around. I'll buy more of a particular fabric if it's a great color that I think I might incorporate into another quilt. It's maddening to run out of the perfect fabric in the middle of a project and not be able to find more, so it's better to overestimate than not have enough.

Prepare Your Fabrics ··················

With your fabric palette selected, the next step is to get the fabrics ready so you can begin "painting." This section will deal with cutting the background fabric and applying fusible web to the remaining fabrics.

· *Prewashing your Fabrics—Or Not* ·

I don't prewash my fabrics because I like them crisp; the sizing added by most manufacturers during the finishing process generally gives them that characteristic. I normally do not have a problem using unwashed fabrics if they are good-quality quilting fabrics, although I have found that the fusible web adheres better to fabric that has had the sizing removed. Try to always buy good-quality fabric. Nothing is worse than having your quilt fade because you bought a low-grade fabric. I realize that some of you prefer to wash and iron your fabrics before use and that's perfectly fine. Do what makes you happy. I'm usually in a hurry to begin working on my next project and sometimes all the prep work gets in the way of my creative flow. If you do decide to prewash your fabrics, do not add fabric softener to the water or use a fabric-softener sheet in the dryer. Those products also will interfere with the fusible web adhering to the fabrics.

· *Cutting the Background Piece* ·

The shape of your quilt will be determined by the shape of your original picture, which should be the shape of your enlarged drawing. Cut your background fabric so it's the same size as the enlarged drawing. You can always crop your quilt later, but you should begin with a piece that is the same shape as the picture.

If you're using more than one fabric for the background, overlap the edges of the fabrics ½". Follow the manufacturer's instructions to fuse them together with a strip of Steam-A-Seam 2 that's cut ½" wide by the length of the fabric.

*Piece background fabrics together
with a strip of fusible web.*

For the patterns given in the book, a suggested enlargement percentage is given. You can change this to fit your personal needs and cut your background fabric accordingly. I like to tackle large-sized quilts, but a friend of mine really likes miniatures. If you're not sure, start small and work up.

· *Applying the Fusible Web* ·

Follow these instructions for each of the fabrics in your palette, with the exception of the background piece. To eliminate wrinkles in your fabrics, iron all of them before applying the fusible web.

1. From the selected yardage, cut a piece of fabric that you think will be large enough for all of the required pieces using that fabric. You can always

prepare more fabric later if needed. A good size to begin with is 9" x 18", which is half of a fat quarter.

2. Cut a piece of Steam-A-Seam 2 that is slightly smaller than the piece of fabric you cut in step 1. Remove one of the paper backings (it doesn't matter which one) and lay the sticky side against the wrong side of the fabric, leaving ⅛" of fabric around the fusible web. The fusible web should not go all the way to the edge. This will protect your iron and ironing board.

3. Using a hot, dry iron, press the fusible web onto the fabric, leaving the iron in one place for approximately 5 to 6 seconds. When you are finished pressing and the fabric has cooled, peel up one corner of the paper backing and make sure the web is properly adhered. If the web hasn't stuck, your iron may not be hot enough. You want the adhesive to penetrate the fibers to prevent the edge of your appliqué pieces from raveling.

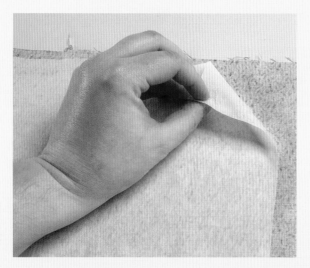

Peel up one corner of the paper backing and make sure the fusible web is properly adhered.

4. Cut off the fabric around the edges, removing a small amount of the fusible web as well. This ensures that the fusible web goes all the way to the edges of your fabric. Leave the paper backing in place.

Trim away the excess fabric and a small amount of the fusible web.

Make and Apply the Appliqués...........

With all of the prep work done, it's time to make your appliqués and apply them to your background. This is where your quilt finally begins to take shape. For this step, you'll need the enlarged drawing of your picture and the original photo.

Remember when you were selecting fabrics and I told you to think of the picture as three-dimensional? You'll need to apply that same concept when you position the appliqués, so it is easiest if you make the appliqués in that order (bottom layer to top) as well. Start by making the shapes that will be fused closest to the background fabric and work toward the ones in the foreground. Again, nothing is permanent until you iron it in place, so if you need to add an appliqué under another shape you can.

1. Lay a piece of freezer paper or tracing paper over the enlarged pattern. You will only be tracing a few shapes at a time, so the paper only needs to be as big as the pieces you want to trace. Using

your ultra-fine-point Sharpie marker, trace the desired shapes onto the paper, leaving some space between shapes. Roughly cut out each shape.

Trace a few shapes at a time onto the paper.

2. Referring to the photo, pin each shape to the *right side* of the fabric that you've chosen for that shape. Cut it out, following the shape of the piece. If you don't pin the freezer-paper shape to the right side of the fabric, it will be reversed when you position it on the background. Do not try and trace the shape onto the paper side of the fabric's fusible web or you'll get the same result. Remove the freezer-paper pattern.

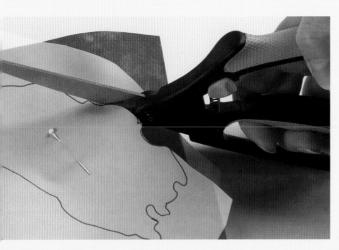

Pin the paper shape to the right side of the fabric and cut it out.

3. Remove the paper backing and stick the appliqué to the background fabric using the enlarged drawing as a guide.

Use the enlarged drawing as a placement guide when positioning the appliqués.

4. Repeat steps 1–3 until all of the appliqué pieces have been cut out and applied to the background. When you are satisfied with the placement of all of the appliqués, use a hot, dry iron to fuse them in place.

RENEGADE THREAD PLAY

IT'S TIME TO DELVE into the second phase of developing your fabric art. At this point you're probably thinking that your quilt top doesn't look quite finished, and you're right—but a little thread painting is going to take care of that. "Renegade Thread Play" is my painting-with-thread technique that adds highlights, shading, and details to Cutting-Garden quilts. Instead of using paint and a paintbrush, you'll be using thread and your sewing machine to draw in fine details, like the veins in a leaf or the sparkle where the light hits the edge of a petal.

It's essentially free-motion quilting with a twist. Like free-motion quilting, you'll be securing the layers together. The twist is that you use heavier thread, and lots of it!

Like the appliqué portion of the process, thread painting involves a series of steps. You'll start by layering your quilt top, batting, and backing, and then move onto the actual stitching. Along the way, I've given you lots of information, so be sure to read through this section to achieve the best results.

Gather Your Supplies ....

With the exception of your iron, ironing board, rotary ruler, and rotary cutter, the supplies you needed for the appliqué process can now be put away and replaced with the following materials. Many of your exact needs will not be able to be determined until you make your test samples, but this will give you a general idea of what to have on hand.

Backing fabric. Your backing fabric is very important to the overall look of your quilt. Although it's easier to use whatever you have lying around or can find cheaply, it's necessary to take your time and pick the right fabric. The right fabric will allow your stitches to blend softly into the print; the wrong fabric will make your stitches more visible than you'd like, even if they are on the back of the quilt. Believe me, I know.

Stay away from solid-colored fabrics and printed fabrics with large open areas. These fabrics tend to show every stitch and unless your stitches are perfect, that probably isn't what you want. Fabrics with a strong color contrast or a geometric print also tend to be bad choices.

Fabrics with strong color contrast, large areas of background showing, and geometric prints are not good backing choices.

Good fabric choices generally convey the same feeling and coloration as the front of your quilt. Large floral and leaf prints are good options. Make sure the motifs are close together and that there isn't a lot of background showing. And even if you think you've selected the right fabric, always make a test sample before you layer your quilt, just to be sure.

Pick a fabric with a print that has great color and no open spaces.

Batting. There are a variety of batting choices available and many are suitable, but I prefer good-quality low-loft cotton batting, like Quilter's Dream Cotton batting (Request Loft) or Warm and Natural. A low-loft batting creates a flat finished quilt and it's easier to fit under the needle while I'm quilting it. Remember, your quilt will be hanging on a wall, so you want the batting to provide a nice, flat look. A batting that drapes, like you would use in a bed quilt, may not lie as flat as you'd like against a wall. Again, a test sample will help you determine if you've made the right choice.

Sewing machine. You don't need a fancy machine to do thread painting, but you must be able to drop the feed dogs so that you can free-motion quilt. Your machine should also be in good working order. Nothing can rob you of the joy of sewing faster than a machine that isn't "feeling well." If you haven't cleaned and oiled it in a while, now would be a good time to do that. Take it to your machine dealer for a professional cleaning or consult your owner's manual for general cleaning and oiling instructions.

Thread. Just like fusible web is the most important supply in the appliqué process, thread is the most important supply in the thread-painting process. You will need thread for the top and the bobbin.

For the top thread, I use Sulky 30-weight rayon. The thickness creates a bolder statement than 40-weight, which is a thinner thread, but if you can't find 30-weight, then 40-weight will work. Pick colors that you find in the flowers, leaves, and background of your quilt. Value is as important here as it was when selecting fabrics, so make sure you have light, medium, and dark values in your thread assortment. Variegated threads of one color family are wonderful because the values are all represented and you don't have to buy as much thread or change your thread as often, but they won't work for everything.

30-weight rayon thread gives a nice shimmer to the project.

The bobbin thread should be lighter weight than the top thread and match your backing fabric, but sometimes your machine will determine the weight of the thread (for more on this, see "Adjust the Thread Tension" on page 43). I like to use a 50-weight cotton thread because I can wind a lot on my bobbin, which keeps me from having to stop as often to reload. If I'm having difficulty achieving the correct tension, I often end up using the same thread in the bobbin that I'm using in the top. You'll find out what works best when you make your test samples.

Sewing-machine needles. Using the correct needle is important in order to keep your thread from shredding and breaking. When you paint with thread, the thread moves quickly through the eye of the needle. A size 90/14 or 80/12 jeans/denim or topstitch needle has a big enough eye to keep the rayon thread intact. Be sure to always start with a new needle and change it as soon as your stitch quality lessens or you begin to experience thread breakage.

Scissors. A pair of small curved-tip scissors or embroidery scissors is helpful when clipping threads close to the quilt top.

Safety pins. Safety pins are used to baste the quilt sandwich together. Medium to medium-large pins work best because they will go through all of the layers and are easier to remove as you're stitching.

Quilting gloves. This is a product that I personally like because the gloves help me control the movement of the quilt as I'm thread painting. There are lots of products on the market for this purpose, so you may already use something different.

For greater control, consider using quilting gloves.

Free-motion presser foot. To do free-motion quilting, you need a free-motion foot or darning foot. If you don't have one, check with your sewing-machine dealer. Make sure the foot opening is large enough that you can see through it clearly while sewing. An open-toe foot looks like it would work, but it isn't a good option because the fabric edges and threads tend to catch on the toes.

*Use an embroidery or darning foot (left)
or a free-motion foot (right) for thread painting.*

Assemble the Layers.....................

Give your quilt top a good steam pressing from both the right and wrong sides. By pressing from both sides, you'll ensure that the appliqués are completely adhered through all the layers. Then use your rotary ruler and cutter to make sure all of the edges of the quilt top are even and the corners are square. Once that is done, you can layer your quilt top, batting, and backing just like you would a traditional quilt. Your backing and batting should be at least 2" larger on all sides than your quilt top. Baste the layers together with safety pins, placing the pins about 8" apart.

Adjust the Thread Tension...............

Before you can begin the renegade thread process, it's essential that you adjust your machine's tension. Sewing machines have their tensions set at the factory to give you perfect tension for using the same thread in the top and the bobbin. If you're using different-weight threads, which you'll most likely be doing when thread painting, you need to adjust your tension. This will not hurt your machine. The key is to have equal thread tension on the front and back of your quilt.

Your tension dial has a mark at the number that indicates the neutral position (usually four or five). If you turn the dial to a greater number you will tighten the top thread. If you turn the dial to a lesser number, you will loosen the top thread. (The bobbin tension is controlled from the bobbin case and we aren't going to mess with it.) Because you are using a heavier thread in the needle than the bobbin during "Renegade Thread Play," you need to loosen the top thread. Don't worry if you are all the way down to one or zero. The important thing is that your tension is even.

How do you know if the tension is even? If you see little dots of bobbin thread showing on the front of your quilt, your top tension is too tight. Loosen it one number at a time until you no longer see the bobbin thread on the quilt top. If you've adjusted your tension as much as possible and can still see dots of bobbin thread on the front, you may need to change the weight of the bobbin thread. You can usually achieve good results with a thread weight that is the same as the top thread. If you still are having difficulty achieving an even tension, try using a different size or type of needle.

It's more important that you don't see any bobbin thread on the front, but you also don't want to see any top thread on the back, if possible. Top thread showing on the back means that your top tension is too loose. Tighten it one number at a time until you no longer see the top thread.

Paint with Thread......................

This section will take you through the actual how-tos of thread painting—where to start and stop, how to add the thread to give the appliqués a realistic look, and so on. The best thing you can do before working on your actual quilt is to spend time practicing the techniques on a test "sandwich." Fuse a few leaf and flower shapes to a piece of leftover background fabric and layer it with the actual backing and batting you're using for your project. Practicing allows you to work out the kinks in your tension and get used to the rhythm of free-motion quilting. When you're comfortable with the process, then start on your quilt.

1. Attach the free-motion presser foot to your machine and insert the needle that will give you the correct tension with the thread you will be using.

2. The first thing you will do is tack down the edges of all of your appliqués. You are going to begin in the middle of your quilt. Thread the needle with a thread color that will blend with the first appliqué shape.

3. Roll up one side of your quilt so that it fits comfortably under the arm of your machine. Slide the flat part of your quilt under the machine so that the needle is over the appliqué you will be tacking.

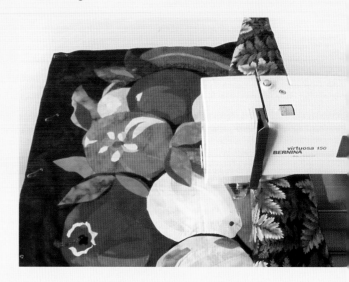

Roll up extra bulk.

4. Drop the machine's feed dogs. The feed dogs are the little teeth that you see under the throat plate. They guide the fabric through the machine when you are sewing. Because you will be guiding the fabric in the direction you want to go, rather than the machine, you must disengage them. Put the presser-foot lever down. If you have a needle-down option on your machine, engage it.

5. Using the hand wheel, insert the needle into the edge of the appliqué and bring the needle back up. This will bring up a loop of the bobbin thread. Pull up the bobbin thread to the top of the quilt. Hold onto the top and bobbin threads and take a few stitches in place, then cut off both thread tails close to the quilt surface. If you follow this process each time you start with a new thread, you will eliminate an unsightly thread nest on the back of your quilt.

Bring up a loop of bobbin thread . . .

. . . and then pull the bobbin thread to the surface.

6. Sew around the edges of the appliqué, guiding the quilt in the direction you want to stitch and removing the safety pins as you approach them. Try to keep your stitch length consistent, but use a longer stitch length than you normally would when free-motion quilting. Your hands should move at about the same rate as the needle. Beginning free-motion quilters often think they have to stitch at a fast and furious pace, but the only thing they achieve is freaking themselves out. If you begin stitching at a rate that makes you uncomfortable, take your foot off the control pedal. Start again, slowly, and stitch steadily. After you stitch for a bit, you will get a rhythm going. Don't be afraid to take out stitches you don't like. You'll be happier in the long run.

7. When you are finished tacking the first appliqué in place, stop with the needle down in the fabric. Lift the presser foot; then use the hand wheel to raise your needle to its highest position. Pull the quilt toward you so you can see where you quit stitching. Tug gently on the top thread to bring up a loop of the bobbin thread. Clip off the top thread and bobbin loop all at once. This will again eliminate a thread nest from forming on the back of your quilt.

Snip the bobbin loop and top thread at the same time.

8. Continue tacking down the edges of the remaining appliqués, working out toward the edges of the quilt. Change the thread color as needed for each appliqué. When you are done with the unrolled area under the machine, roll it up and work on the remaining portion of the quilt in the same manner.

9. Now it's time to add shadows, highlights, and other thread details. This is the time to add any details that you couldn't add with fabric. For this part, you will work on the appliqués closest to the outside edges first, and then move toward the center of the quilt. Work in small sections at a time, and focus only on the part under your presser foot as you're stitching. Go over the area as much as you need to create the effect you're looking for. Change the thread color as often as needed to create the desired effect. Use darker thread for shadows and lighter thread for highlights.

When you are working on petals, follow the curvature of the shape. This will make the petals look like they are bending over. If it helps, use a chalk pencil to draw in the lines first.

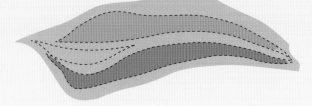

For leaves, use thread to create the veins, as well as to add the highlights and shadows.

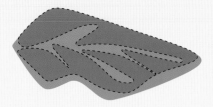

10. Quilt the background last. I like to use a simple echo stitch. To do this, use a thread that matches your background fabric. Follow the lines of the appliqués lying against the background. Stitch a presser-foot width away from the appliqués. Then, without lifting your needle or cutting your threads, stitch a presser-foot width away from the last line of stitching. Continue in the manner until you reach the outside edge of your quilt.

Using an echo stitch in the background gives a clean look.

STICKY SOLUTION

It is inevitable that you will get a sticky buildup on your needle during the thread-painting process. The buildup will eventually interfere with your stitch quality, so eliminate it often. I have two solutions for getting rid of it. The first one won't cost you a dime and it's always handy: saliva. Just put a little on your finger and rub it over the needle. You'll be amazed at how easily the sticky stuff comes off. I also use a product called Thread Heaven, which has a silicone base. It's actually a thread conditioner but it removes buildup well. Just pinch off a little ball of the conditioner and rub it on your needle. The adhesive will come right off. Don't worry about the little bit of conditioner that might still be on the needle; it will keep the buildup from occurring quite as fast. For both methods, be careful that you don't get your finger caught on the tip of the needle and cut yourself.

FINISHING TOUCHES

LIKE ALL ARTISTIC WORKS, Cutting-Garden quilts require you to take some steps before you can hang your project and enjoy it. Along with some of the supplies you used to appliqué and quilt your project, you will also need a walking foot, T pins, and fabrics for making a hanging sleeve and label.

Press the Quilt Top

When the thread painting is completed, press your quilt with a hot steam iron from the front and the back. As well as helping the quilt to lie flat, pressing from both sides helps embed the threads in the quilt. It also reactivates the glue in the fusible web to adhere it to the threads so that the threads also become fused to the quilt.

Square it Up

Even though you squared up your quilt top once already, the quilting process makes it necessary to do it again to remove any bits of fabric and batting that may be hanging over the edges. This is also a great time to assess your work and see what finished size you would like your quilt to be. Maybe you don't like that leaf that's on one side, or maybe you want the finished quilt to be a square shape rather than rectangular. Use your rotary cutter and ruler to take care of these issues; make sure your edges are even and your corners are square.

Attach a Hanging Sleeve

Cutting-Garden quilts are meant to hang on a wall so you will need to attach a hanging sleeve to the backing. I attach my sleeves before the binding is sewn on.

1. Measure the width of your squared-up quilt. Cut a piece of the sleeve fabric that is 10" wide by the width of your quilt.

2. Press under the short ends of the sleeve piece ¼", and then another ½", to create a hem. Sew the hem in place.

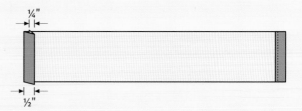

3. Fold the hemmed sleeve piece in half lengthwise, wrong sides together; press.

4. With the raw edges aligned, center the sleeve at the top edge of the your quilt. Pin it in place. Using a walking foot, baste across the top of the sleeve, ¼" from the edges. (The binding will cover the raw edges.)

5. Pin the folded edge of the sleeve to the quilt. With matching thread, blind stitch the folded edge of the sleeve to the quilt, making sure you do not stitch through to the front of the quilt.

Add the Binding

1. From your binding fabric, cut 2½"-wide strips. You will need enough strips to go around the outside of the quilt plus an additional 10" for seams and mitered corners.

2. With right sides together, join the strips on the diagonal as shown to make one continuous strip. Trim the seam allowances to ¼" and press the seam allowances open.

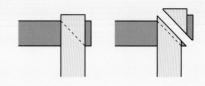

3. Cut one end of the pieced strip at a 45° angle and press it under ¼". Press the strip in half lengthwise, wrong sides together.

Fold line

4. Beginning with the angled end, pin the binding to one edge of the front side of the quilt. Using your walking foot and a ¼" seam allowance, stitch the binding to the first side, beginning about 8" from the angled end and ending ¼" from the first corner. Backstitch, remove the quilt from under the needle, and clip the threads.

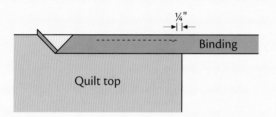

¼"

Binding

Quilt top

5. Turn the quilt so that you will be stitching down the next side. Fold the binding straight up and then back down onto itself, keeping the corner square and the raw edges even. Begin stitching at the edge and stop stitching ¼" from the next corner. Repeat the folding and stitching process at each corner.

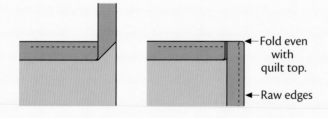

Fold even with quilt top.

Raw edges

6. Stop stitching about 2" from the starting point of the binding. Trim the end of the binding so it overlaps the beginning about 2", trimming diagonally. Tuck the end of the binding inside the beginning of the binding and finish sewing the binding in place.

7. Fold the binding over the raw edge of the quilt to the back. Blind stitch the folded edge in place, mitering the corners.

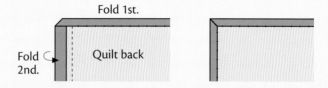

Fold 1st.

Fold 2nd.

Quilt back

Block the Quilt

This step will ensure that your finished quilt is square and the edges hang straight. Place your quilt on your design board. Secure it in place with T pins, making sure the quilt is square and lies flat against the board. Gently pull on the quilt if needed to make this happen. Using a spray bottle, spritz your quilt top with water. It doesn't need to be dripping wet, but it should be more than a light misting. Let it sit for a few hours and then lightly iron it with a steam iron while it is still on the board. Let the quilt dry thoroughly before removing it from the board.

Label Your Quilt

You want future generations to know about this beautiful piece of art, so it is important to label your quilt with its name, your name, and the date you completed it. It's also fun to put what inspired you to make the quilt and your thoughts while making it. Your family will truly enjoy this little extra step.

Care for Your Finished Quilt

I get asked all the time if these quilts can be washed. Yes, they can, but why? This is an art quilt. Would you wash your Picasso? If necessary, immerse your quilt in cold water and let it air-dry. Give it a good steam pressing and it should look as good as new.

If you need to store your quilt, rolling it onto something is better than folding it. I wrap a foam swimming-pool "noodle" with batting and then fabric, and then roll my quilt onto it so that the quilt backing is facing out. Wrapping it in this manner prevents the quilt from lying directly against the foam, which may be made from chemicals that could harm the quilt. I then place the tube on a shelf away from direct sunlight.

CUTTING~GARDEN QUILTS

THESE PROJECTS ARE FOR those of you who want to experience the Cutting-Garden technique without all the thinking that goes into developing your own pattern. Although many of the steps have been eliminated, you will still need to refer to some of the sections in "Fabulous Fusible Appliqué" on page 29, so be sure you consult those areas when indicated in the instructions. When it comes to the thread-painting part, you will need to be familiar with all of the sections of "Renegade Thread Play," beginning on page 40.

Each pattern comes with an outline drawing that's ready to be enlarged and a fabric key indicating what fabric to use for each appliqué shape. The enlargement percentage given on each pattern will make a quilt that's the finished size indicated at the beginning of the project. Feel free to increase or decrease this percentage to make a different-sized quilt, but be aware that the yardages given for the fabrics and batting may change.

The fabric key gives the number or letter that corresponds to each appliqué shape that will be cut from that fabric on the pattern. It also lists the yardage needed for each appliqué and background fabric used. Other fabrics and supplies that you need are given in the materials listing.

Each quilt's fabric key serves only as a suggestion for which fabrics to use. These are the fabrics that I used to make the quilt you see in the picture given with each project. It is helpful to use the key when shopping for fabrics, but you probably won't find the exact fabrics I used. Use the key instead as a reference for where to place the light, medium, and dark fabrics. If you want to change the color of your flower entirely, the fabric key can still be helpful in deciding where to place the different values.

Selecting fabrics is often the hardest part of the process, but don't panic. Usually your first instinct is right. If you're still unsure, ask a friend whose color choices you respect for help, or ask the people who work at the quilt shop. Quilt shops usually hire very creative people and most of them are always willing to take the time to help a fellow quilter. The patterns become progressively more difficult. "Clematis" on page 52 is the easiest because it uses the fewest pieces; I've also broken down the pattern into background and foreground shapes for you. I suggest starting with it so you can get a feel for the process before you tackle one of the more complex patterns, such as "Peach Rose" on page 86.

CLEMATIS

The deep, rich colors of the clematis are intense, from its smooth, folded petals to its large leaves. I love the odd spiky stamen in the center. It reminds me of a swirling skirt on a purple dance floor. This quilt is a great place to use a variety of fabrics from the blue and violet families.

FINISHED QUILT SIZE: 28" x 21½"

Materials...............................

In addition to the materials listed here, you will also need the fabrics listed in the fabric key on page 57. For more information on basic supplies, see pages 29 and 41.

⅓ yard of fabric for binding

1 yard of fabric for backing

1 yard of batting

5 yards of 18"-wide Steam-A-Seam 2

Freezer paper or tracing paper

Black ultra-fine-point Sharpie marker

Size 90/14 jeans/denim needle or topstitch needle

30-weight rayon thread in colors to match flower, leaf, and background fabrics

Assemble the Quilt Top...................

1. Enlarge patterns 1 and 2 on pages 58 and 59 the percentage indicated.

2. From the background fabric, cut a 23" x 30" rectangle. Place it on your design board.

3. Refer to "Prepare Your Fabrics" on page 37 to apply Steam-A-Seam 2 to fabrics A–V.

4. Using the pattern 1 enlargement and referring to "Make and Apply the Appliqués" on page 38, make the pattern pieces for the leaf shapes that are behind the flower shapes. Transfer the letter to each pattern as you trace it. Refer to the fabric key and use the patterns to cut out the appliqués from the prepared fabrics. Remove the paper backing from the appliqués and stick them to the

background fabric where indicated on the pattern. Do not iron them in place yet. The background fabric is cut slightly larger to allow for squaring up the top later. Keep this in mind as you position the appliqués.

5. Repeat step 4 to make the petal appliqués and apply them to the background fabric. Add the yellow centers.

6. Using pattern 2, add the appliqués that create the highlights, which are the lighter fabrics, and the shadows that are the darker fabrics. Add the stem appliqués.

7. Make and apply the remaining two pieces for the center of each flower. Cut thin strips from fabrics M and N and apply them around the flower centers as shown.

Pattern 1 pieces arranged on the background fabric.

8. When you are satisfied with the arrangement of all of the appliqués, press the quilt top to permanently adhere the pieces.

Shadows, highlights, and stems from pattern 2 added to the pattern 1 appliqués.

Add Thread Details...................

Refer to "Renegade Thread Play" on page 40 for thread-painting specifics.

1. Layer the quilt top with batting and backing. Use safety pins to baste the layers together.

2. Add thread-painting details to the petals first. Follow the flow of the petals with your thread. This will make the petals look like they are bending over. Use a darker thread where the petals are darker to give the look of shadow. Use a lighter thread where the petals are lighter to reinforce the highlighting.

3. Move to the flower centers. Accent the shape of the existing pieces and add more spikey details around the outer edges, curving some of the lines. This is a good place to use two colors of thread, such as yellow and lime green, to add more depth.

4. Add the thread details to the leaves, referring to the photo on pages 52 and 53 for ideas.

5. Quilt the background areas last.

Finish with Flair ....

Refer to "Finishing Touches" on page 48 to press the quilted piece, square it up, attach a hanging sleeve, bind the edges, block the bound quilt, and add a label.

Thread details added to the flower centers.

Fabric Key ....

Background		⅞ yard	**L**		Fat quarter
A		Fat quarter	**M**		⅛ yard
B		½ yard	**N**		⅛ yard
C		½ yard	**O**		⅛ yard
D		Fat quarter	**P**		Fat quarter
E		Fat quarter	**Q**		Fat quarter
F		Fat quarter	**R**		Fat quarter
G		Fat quarter	**S**		Fat quarter
H		Fat quarter	**T**		½ yard
I		Fat quarter	**U**		Fat quarter
J		Fat quarter	**V**		⅛ yard
K		Fat quarter			

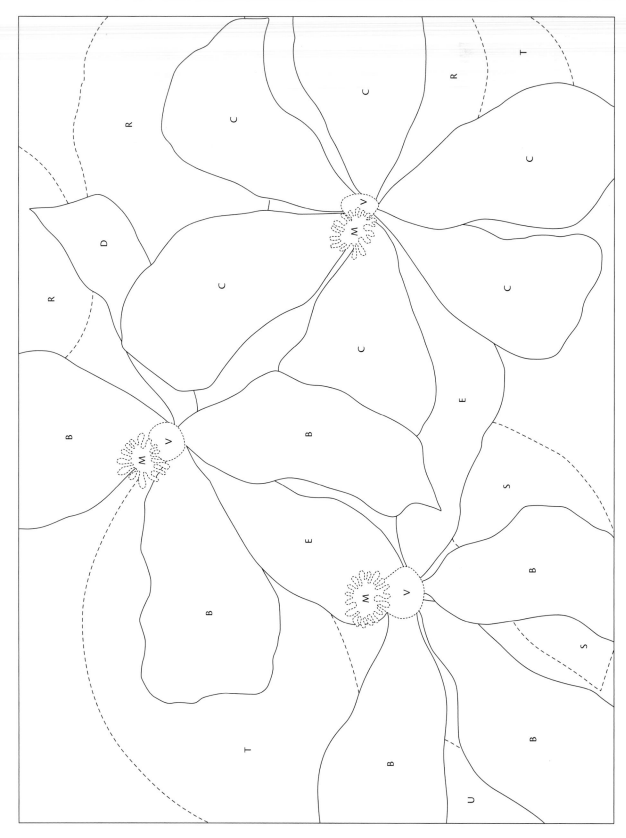

Clematis
Pattern 1.
Enlarge 333%.

Clematis
Pattern 2.
Enlarge 333%.

CONEFLOWER

Just picked from the garden and ready for the bud vase, these brightly colored coneflowers are a fun and easy way to try the Cutting-Garden technique. Substitute different fabrics and these coneflowers can easily be transformed into daisies or black-eyed Susans.

FINISHED QUILT SIZE: 18" x 22"

Materials......................................

In addition to the materials listed here, you will also need the fabrics listed in the fabric key on page 64. For more information on basic supplies, see pages 29 and 41.

⅓ yard of fabric for border

⅓ yard of fabric for binding

⅝ yard of fabric for backing

⅝ yard of batting

3 yards of 18"-wide Steam-A-Seam 2

Freezer paper or tracing paper

Black ultra-fine-point Sharpie marker

Size 90/14 jeans/denim needle or topstitch needle

30-weight rayon thread in colors to match flower, leaf, and background fabrics

Assemble the Quilt Top...................

1. Enlarge the pattern on page 65 the percentage indicated.

2. From the background fabric, cut a 20" x 24" rectangle. Place it on your design board.

3. Refer to "Prepare Your Fabrics" on page 37 to apply Steam-A-Seam 2 to fabrics A–L.

4. Using the enlarged pattern and referring to "Make and Apply the Appliqués" on page 38, make the pattern pieces for the flower centers. Transfer the letter to each pattern as you trace it. Refer to the fabric key and use the patterns to cut out the appliqués from the prepared fabrics. Remove the paper backing from the appliqués and stick them to the background rectangle where indicated on the pattern. Do not iron them in place yet. The background fabric is cut slightly larger to allow for squaring up the top later. Keep this in mind as you position the appliqués.

5. Trace the full-sized patterns on pages 66 and 67 onto freezer paper or tracing paper. Transfer the letter and number to each shape as you trace it. The dashed lines represent overlapping pieces; you do not need to transfer these lines. Refer

to the fabric key and use the patterns to cut out the appliqués from the prepared fabric that corresponds to each shape's letter. Remove the paper backing from the appliqués. Using the enlarged pattern as a guide, stick the appliqués to the background rectangle in the location that corresponds to the number on each appliqué. The flower centers should butt up to or slightly overlap the flower petals. Do not iron the appliqués in place yet.

6. Using the enlarged pattern, repeat step 4 to make the stem and leaf appliqués and apply them to the background fabric.

7. Repeat step 4 to make and apply the appliqués for the petal highlights and shadows.

8. When you are satisfied with the arrangement of all of the appliqués, press the quilt top to permanently adhere the pieces.

Attach the Border.........................

1. Trim the quilt top to the desired size and square up the corners.

2. Measure the quilt-top length through the center. From the border fabric, cut two strips, 2½" wide and the length measured. Sew the strips to the sides of the quilt top. Press the seam allowances toward the border strips.

3. Measure the quilt-top width through the center, including the side borders. From the border fabric, cut two strips, 2½" wide and the length measured. Sew the strips to the top and bottom of the quilt top. Press the seam allowances toward the border strips.

Add Thread Details......................

Refer to "Renegade Thread Play" on page 40 for thread-painting specifics.

1. Layer the quilt top with batting and backing. Use safety pins to baste the layers together.

2. Add thread-painting details to the petals first. Follow the flow of the curve of the petals with

your thread. With a darker thread, go back and add shadows where the petals touch the center of the flowers.

3. Thread paint a zigzag pattern through the flower centers.

4. Add details to the leaves and stems, adding more leaves within the existing leaves and along the stems.

5. Thread paint the background. Use a thread that matches your background fabric to echo stitch, following the lines of the petals and leaves.

6. Quilt the border with straight lines spaced approximately ⅜" apart.

Finish with Flair ························

Refer to "Finishing Touches" on page 48 to press the quilted piece, square it up, attach a hanging sleeve, bind the edges, block the bound quilt, and add a label.

Fabric Key ··

Background		⅝ yard		**G**		Fat quarter
A		⅛ yard		**H**		Fat quarter
B		⅛ yard		**I**		Fat quarter
C		⅛ yard		**J**		Fat quarter
D		Fat quarter		**K**		Fat quarter
E		Fat quarter		**L**		Fat quarter
F		Fat quarter				

Coneflower
Enlarge 200%.

Upper coneflower petals
Patterns are full-size. *Do not enlarge.*

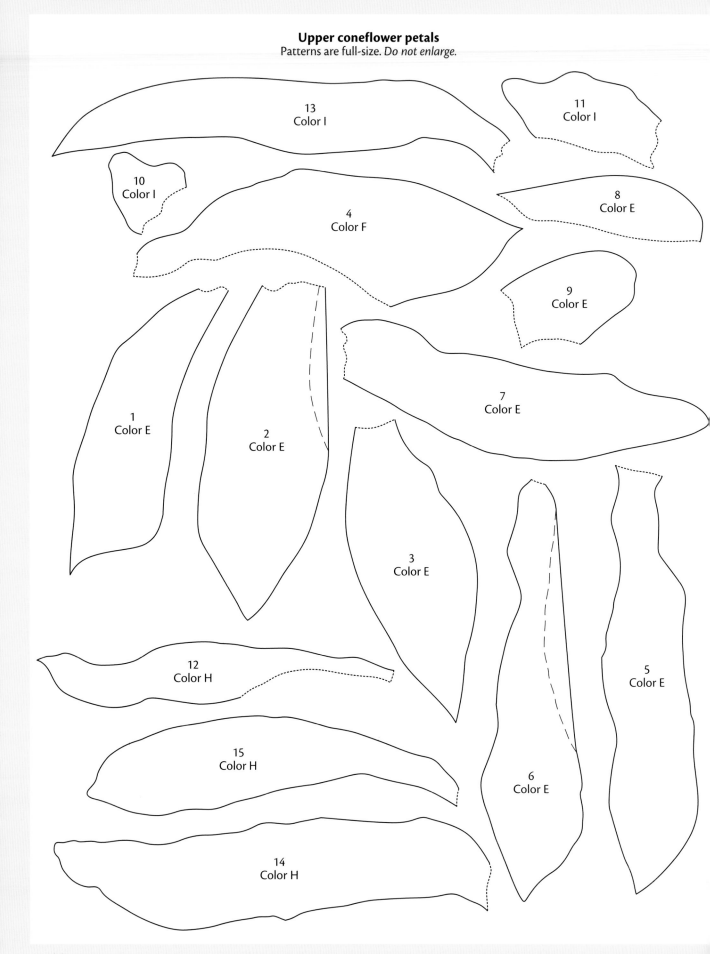

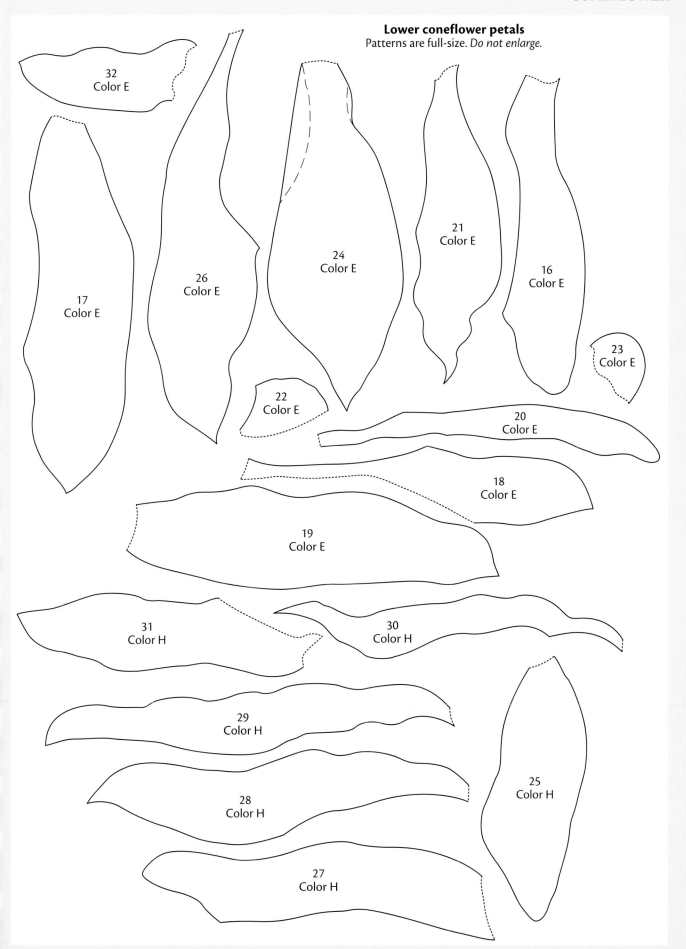

Lower coneflower petals
Patterns are full-size. *Do not enlarge.*

32
Color E

17
Color E

26
Color E

24
Color E

21
Color E

16
Color E

23
Color E

22
Color E

20
Color E

18
Color E

19
Color E

31
Color H

30
Color H

29
Color H

25
Color H

28
Color H

27
Color H

APPLE BOWL

I love the fall season. Nature's colors are changing and it's harvest time at the orchard. Can't you almost smell the sweetness of the apples as you enjoy this vintage wooden bowl full of fruit?

FINISHED QUILT SIZE: 31½" x 26½"

Materials.................................

In addition to the materials listed here, you will also need the fabrics listed in the fabric key on pages 72 and 73. For more information on basic supplies, see pages 29 and 41.

⅜ yard of fabric for binding

1⅛ yards of fabric for backing

1⅛ yards of batting

6 yards of 18"-wide Steam-A-Seam 2

Freezer paper or tracing paper

Black ultra-fine-point Sharpie marker

Size 90/14 jeans/denim needle or topstitch needle

30-weight rayon thread in colors to match fruit, leaf, background, tabletop, and bowl fabrics

Assemble the Quilt Top.................

1. Enlarge the patterns on pages 74 and 75 the percentage indicated. Tape them together to make a complete pattern.

2. From the top background fabric, cut an 18" x 33" rectangle. Cut a 12" x 33" rectangle from the bottom background fabric. With right sides together, stitch the rectangles together along the long edges. Press the seam allowance open. Place the pieced rectangle on your design board so that the green rectangle is above the greenish yellow rectangle. The background fabrics are cut slightly larger to allow for squaring up the top later. Keep this in mind as you position the appliqués.

3. Refer to "Prepare Your Fabrics" on page 37 to apply Steam-A-Seam 2 to fabrics A–Z and 1–12.

4. Using the enlarged pattern and referring to "Make and Apply the Appliqués" on page 38, make the pattern piece for the inside of the bowl (12) as one piece. Cut out the appliqué shape from fabric 12. Remove the paper backing from the appliqué and stick it to the background rectangle as shown. Do not iron it in place yet.

5. Repeat step 4 to make the appliqués for the outside of the bowl and apply them to the background.

6. Make and apply the remaining appliqués, adding the highlights and the shadows to each piece last.

7. When you are satisfied with the arrangement of the appliqués, press the quilt top to permanently adhere the pieces to the background.

Add Thread Details.................

Refer to "Renegade Thread Play" on page 40 for thread-painting specifics.

1. Layer the quilt top with batting and backing. Use safety pins to baste the layers together.

2. Thread paint the fruits, referring to the photo on pages 68 and 69 for ideas. Follow the curve of the apples and match the thread colors to the fruit colors to accent the shadows and highlights.

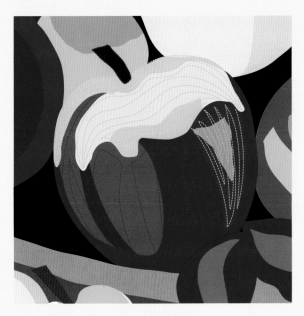

3. Add the thread details to the leaves.

4. Echo stitch the top background fabric. Follow the linear lines of the appliqués to thread paint the table.

Finish with Flair.................

Refer to "Finishing Touches" on page 48 to press the quilted piece, square it up, attach a hanging sleeve, bind the edges, block the bound quilt, and add a label.

Fabric Key...

Top background	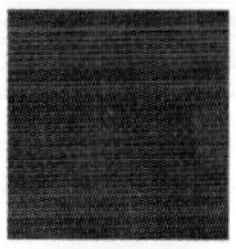	⅝ yard	K		¼ yard
Bottom background	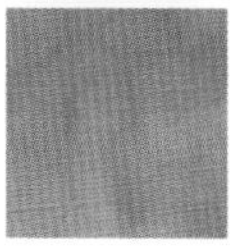	½ yard	L		¼ yard
A		¼ yard	M		¼ yard
B		¼ yard	N		¼ yard
C		¼ yard	O		¼ yard
D		¼ yard	P		¼ yard
E		¼ yard	Q		¼ yard
F		¼ yard	R		¼ yard
G		¼ yard	S		¼ yard
H		¼ yard	T		¼ yard
I		¼ yard	U		¼ yard
J		¼ yard	V	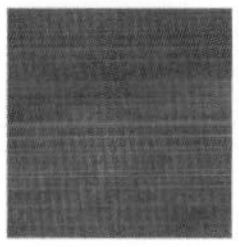	¼ yard

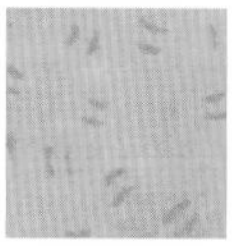

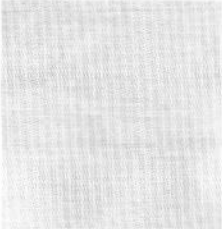

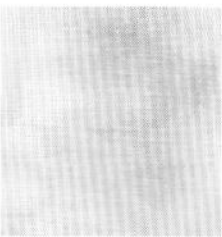

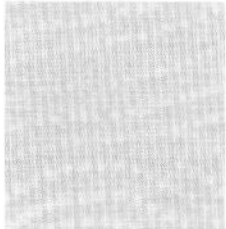

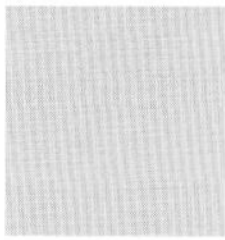

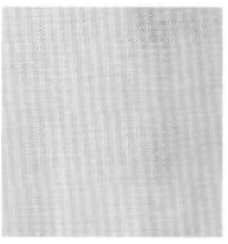

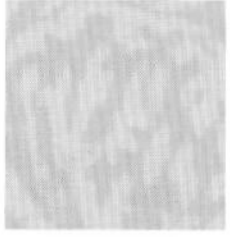

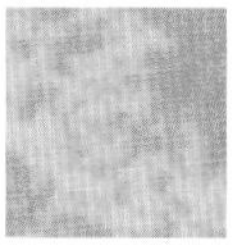

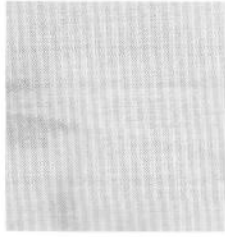

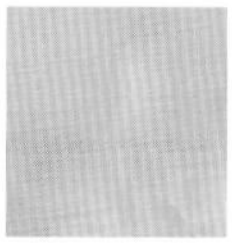

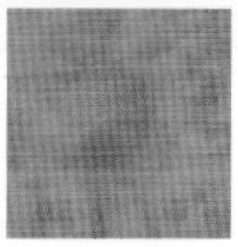

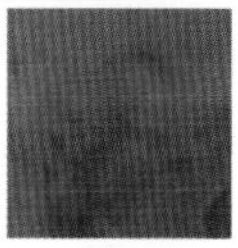

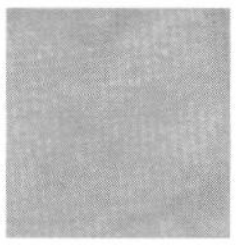

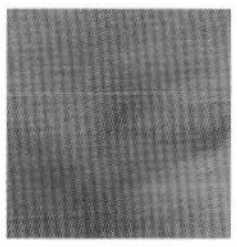

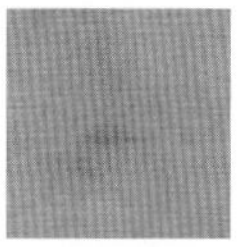

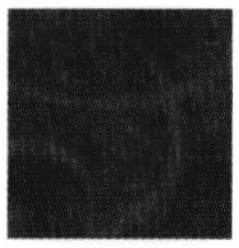

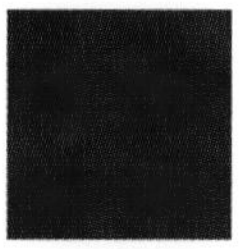

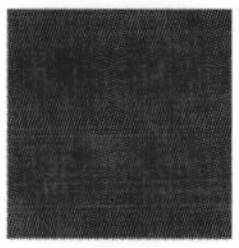

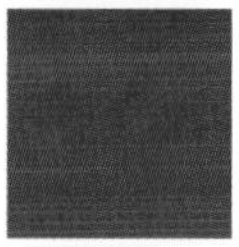

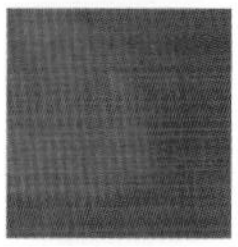

W		¼ yard		5		¼ yard
X		¼ yard		6		½ yard
Y		¼ yard		7		¼ yard
Z		¼ yard		8		¼ yard
1		¼ yard		9		¼ yard
2		¼ yard		10		¼ yard
3		¼ yard		11		¼ yard
4		¼ yard		12		½ yard

Apple Bowl
Enlarge 300%.

Apple Bowl
Enlarge 300%.

PANSIES IN VASE

These delicate little pansies, with their happy, smiling faces, were sitting on my desk in a clear glass vase just waiting to be captured in time forever. Pansies come in a wide variety of colors and this quilt is a wonderful place to try out your favorites.

FINISHED QUILT SIZE: 20¾" x 23½"

Materials ······························

In addition to the materials listed here, you will also need the fabrics listed in the fabric key on pages 80 and 81. For more information on basic supplies, see pages 29 and 41.

⅓ yard of fabric for binding

1 yard of fabric for backing

1 yard of batting

3 yards of 18"-wide Steam-A-Seam 2

Freezer paper or tracing paper

Black ultra-fine-point Sharpie marker

Size 90/14 jeans/denim needle or topstitch needle

30-weight rayon thread in colors to match flower, leaf, background, and vase fabrics

Assemble the Quilt Top ···················

1. Enlarge the patterns on pages 83–85 the percentage indicated.

2. Refer to "Prepare Your Fabrics" on page 37 to apply Steam-A-Seam 2 to fabrics A–Z and fabrics 1–7. Do not apply the fusible web to the background fabrics.

3. Using the enlarged pattern and referring to "Make and Apply the Appliqués" on page 38, make the pattern piece for the table edge (Y). Draw the pattern as one long piece that will go from one side of the quilt to the other. Cut out the appliqué from fabric Y.

4. From the top background fabric, cut a 16" x 24" rectangle. Cut a 12" x 24" rectangle from the bottom background fabric. Butt the long edges of the fabrics together. Remove the paper backing from the table-edge appliqué and center it over the butted edges. Press the appliqué in place to join the background fabrics. Be aware that this is the only time you will press an appliqué in place

before the remaining appliqués are in place. Also, the background piece is slightly larger than the finished quilt to allow for squaring up the quilt top later. Keep this in mind as you position the remaining appliqués. Place the background piece on your design board.

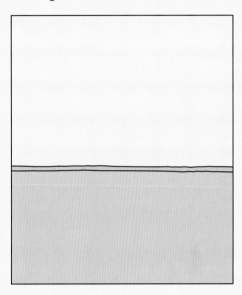

5. Make the appliqués for the table shadows (R) and stick them to the bottom background fabric.

6. Make the pattern pieces for the vase background, highlights, and shadows. Transfer the letter to each pattern as you trace it. Refer to the fabric key and use the patterns to cut out the appliqués from the prepared fabrics. Remove the paper backing from the appliqués and stick them to the background rectangle, beginning with the background(2) and adding the highlights and shadows in the order shown.

7. Repeat step 6 to make the flower and stem appliqués and stick them to the background fabric. Make and apply the largest petals closest to the background first and work your way toward the centers, layering the pieces as you go.

8. Make and apply the leaf appliqués.

9. When you are satisfied with the arrangement of all of the appliqués, press the quilt top to permanently adhere the pieces.

Add Thread Details

Refer to "Renegade Thread Play" on page 40 for thread-painting specifics.

1. Layer the quilt top with batting and backing. Use safety pins to baste the layers together.

2. Add thread-painting details to the vase first. Follow the curve of the pieces with your thread to accentuate the shape of the vase.

3. Using the photo on pages 76 and 77 for ideas, thread paint the flower petals and centers next. Use thread colors that are darker than the fabric around some of the petals to create the illusion of the colors bleeding into each other.

4. Stitch the leaves next, following the shape of some of the leaves and adding veins to others. As you move from leaf to leaf, stitch the stems connecting the leaves and add an occasional loopy tendril.

5. Echo quilt the top background fabric. Add horizontal lines of stitching to the tabletop background.

Finish with Flair

Refer to "Finishing Touches" on page 48 to press the quilted piece, square it up, attach a hanging sleeve, bind the edges, block the bound quilt, and add a label.

Fabric Key

Fabric key is for the quilt shown on page 78.

Top background	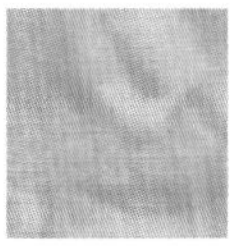	⅝ yard	**F**		⅛ yard
Bottom background	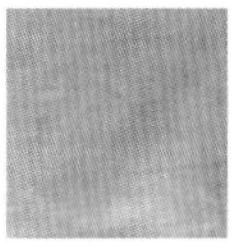	½ yard	**G**		⅛ yard
A	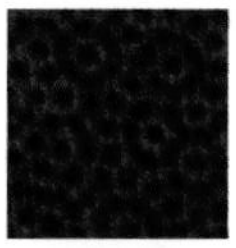	¼ yard	**H**		⅛ yard
B		¼ yard	**I**		¼ yard
C		¼ yard	**J**		¼ yard
D		¼ yard	**K**		¼ yard
E		¼ yard	**L**	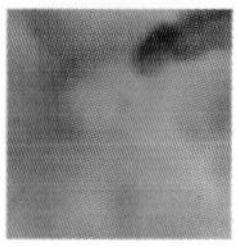	⅛ yard

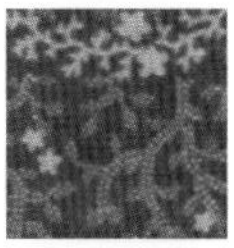

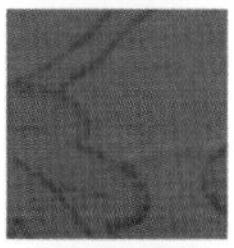

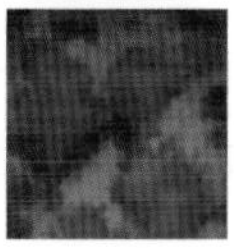

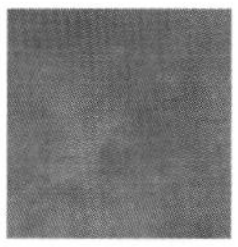

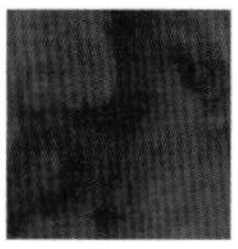

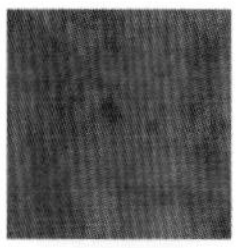

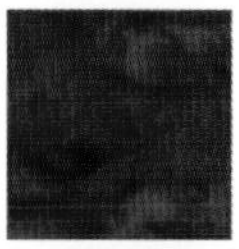

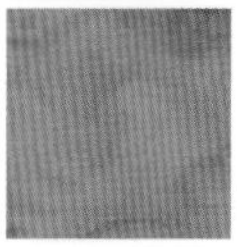

M		⅛ yard	**Y**		⅛ yard
N		⅛ yard	**Z**		⅛ yard
O		⅛ yard	**1**		⅛ yard
P		⅛ yard	**2**		⅛ yard
Q		⅛ yard	**3**		⅛ yard
R		⅛ yard	**4**		⅛ yard
S		⅛ yard	**5**		⅛ yard
T		⅛ yard	**6**		⅛ yard
U		⅛ yard	**7**		⅛ yard
V		⅛ yard			
W		⅛ yard			
X		⅛ yard			

Try a different color palette to create your favorite pansy colors.

Vase highlight and shadow patterns
are on pages 84 and 85.

Pansies in Vase
Enlarge 285%.

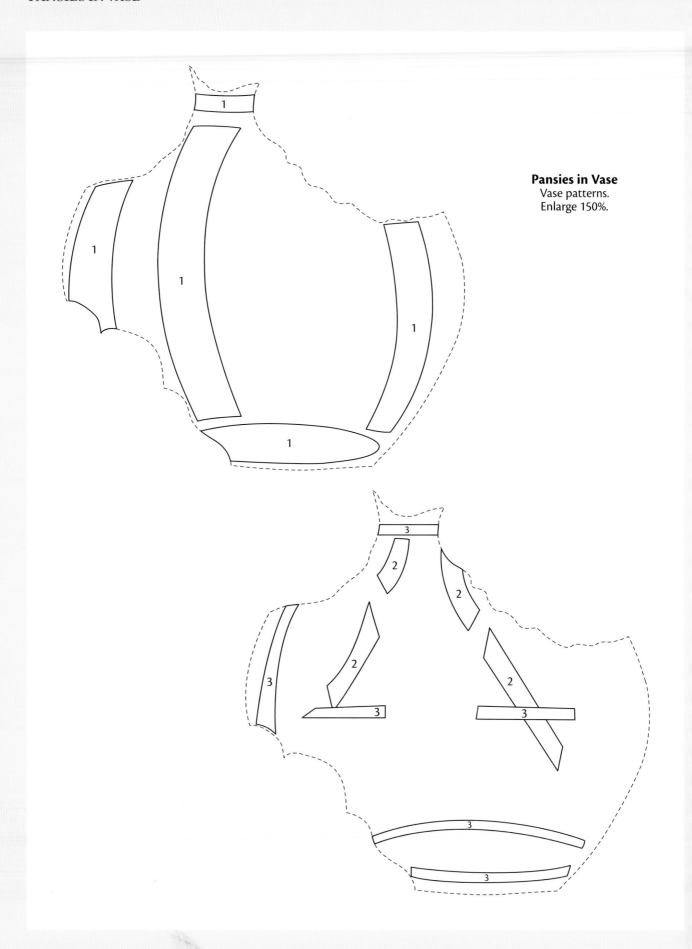

Pansies in Vase
Vase patterns.
Enlarge 150%.

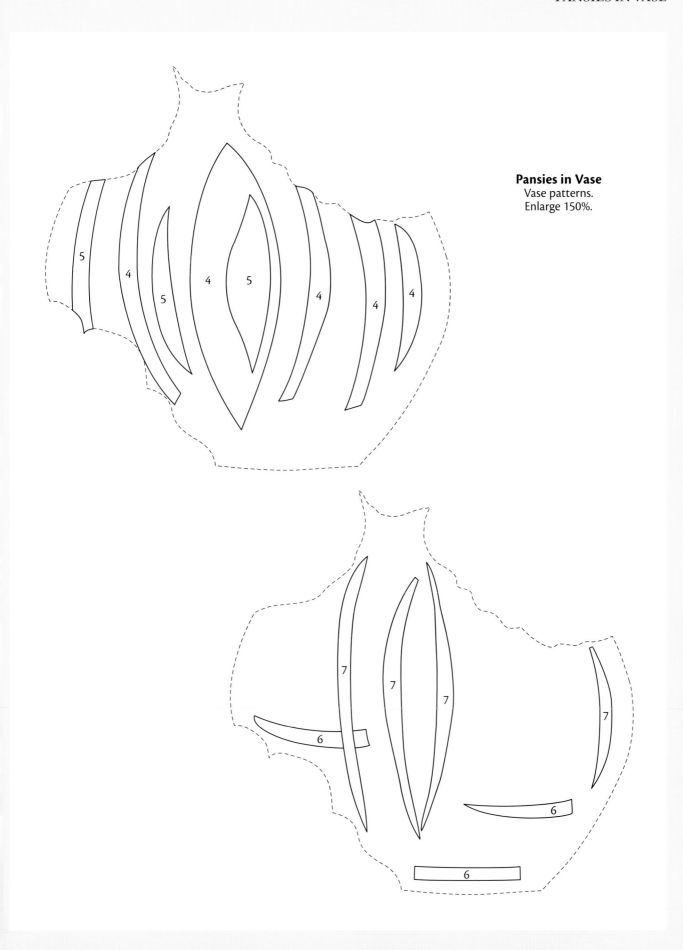

Pansies in Vase
Vase patterns.
Enlarge 150%.

PEACH ROSE

Roses are my favorite flower to both grow and quilt. This rose started out dark red as a bud, but as its petals unfolded the color changed to pinky peach and soft salmon. As it started to fade with time, the tips of the petals turned a light creamy yellow. Creating a rose is sometimes challenging even with a pattern, but you can do it. Because this one includes so many pieces, I've simplified the background so that you will only be working with one fabric. If you want to try and add the leaves and shadows that you see in the photo on your own, go for it!

FINISHED QUILT SIZE: 37" x 34"

Materials . . . .

In addition to the materials listed here, you will also need the fabrics listed in the fabric key on pages 90 and 91. For more information on basic supplies, see pages 29 and 41.

⅜ yard of fabric for binding

1⅓ yards of fabric for backing

1⅓ yards of batting

12 yards of 18"-wide Steam-A-Seam 2

Freezer paper or tracing paper

Black ultra-fine-point Sharpie marker

Size 90/14 jeans/denim needle or topstitch needle

30-weight rayon thread in colors to match flower and background fabrics

Assemble the Quilt Top . . . .

1. Enlarge the patterns on pages 92 and 93 the percentage indicated. Tape the patterns together to make a complete pattern.

2. From the background fabric, cut a 36" x 39" rectangle. Place it on your design board.

3. Refer to "Prepare Your Fabrics" on page 37 to apply Steam-A-Seam 2 to fabrics A–Z and fabric 1.

4. Using the enlarged pattern and referring to "Make and Apply the Appliqués" on page 38, make the pattern pieces for the rose, working outward from the center. Transfer the letter to each pattern as you trace it. Refer to the fabric key and use the patterns to cut out the appliqués from the prepared fabrics. Remove the paper backing from the appliqués and stick them to the background rectangle where indicated on the pattern. Do not iron them in place yet. The background fabric is cut slightly larger to allow for squaring up the top later. Keep this in mind as you position the appliqués. Because this is a large quilt, step back from the quilt top frequently as you are positioning the appliqués to check the overall look.

5. When you are satisfied with the arrangement of all of the appliqués, press the quilt top to permanently adhere the pieces.

Add Thread Details . . . .

Refer to "Renegade Thread Play" on page 40 for thread-painting specifics.

1. Layer the quilt top with batting and backing. Use safety pins to baste the layers together.

2. Add thread-painting details to the petals first. Follow the flow of the petals with your thread. This will make the petals look like they are bending over. Use a darker thread where the petals meet at the base of the rose to give the look of a shadow. Use lighter thread on the ends of the petals to mimic light hitting the petal tips.

3. Echo quilt the background last.

Finish with Flair . . . .

Refer to "Finishing Touches" on page 48 to press the quilted piece, square it up, attach a hanging sleeve, bind the edge, block the bound quilt, and add a label.

Fabric Key..

Background		1¼ yards
A		½ yard
B		½ yard
C		½ yard
D		¼ yard
E		½ yard
F		¼ yard
G		¼ yard

H		½ yard
I		¼ yard
J		1 yard
K		1 yard
L		1 yard
M		½ yard

N		¼ yard
O		¼ yard
P		¼ yard
Q		½ yard
R		¼ yard
S		¼ yard

T		1 yard
U		¼ yard
V		¼ yard
W		½ yard
X		½ yard
Y		½ yard
Z		½ yard
1		½ yard

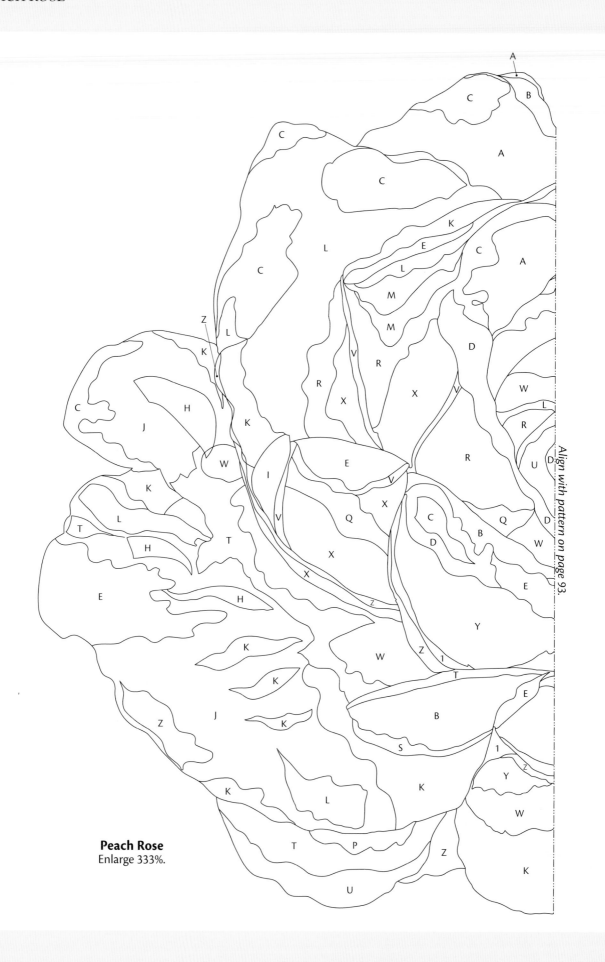

Peach Rose
Enlarge 333%.

Align with pattern on page 93.

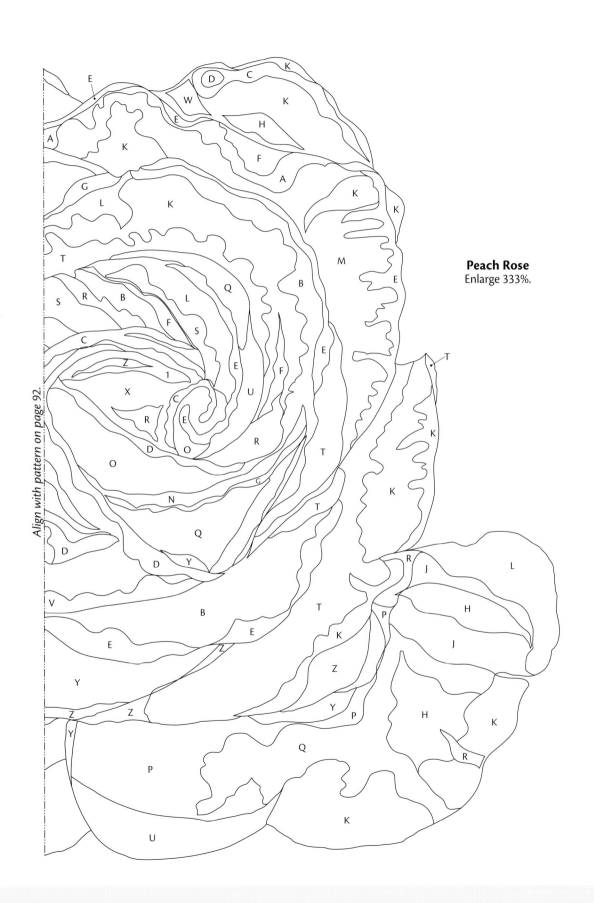

Peach Rose
Enlarge 333%.

Align with pattern on page 92.

RAISED IN SOUTHERN CALIFORNIA, MELINDA BULA has been in love with fabric and sewing since she was a young girl. She made her first quilt in 1976 when she was just out of high school and her second one when she was stationed in Hawaii as a flight attendant. Three years later she moved to San Francisco where she met her husband, Joe.

Educated in art and design, Melinda worked in interior design for 15 years as a fabric and wallpaper designer. She and her husband started their own wallpaper- and fabric-design business soon after the birth of their son, Matthew, in 1988. The company, Melinda Bula Designs, sold hand-silk-screened wallpapers and fabrics nationwide. Melinda's wallpaper and fabric designs have been featured on the cover of several issues of *Better Homes and Gardens* magazine as well as in *Sunset* design books and other noted publications.

Since moving to El Dorado Hills, California, in 1996, Melinda has been involved in quilting and wearable arts. She loves to experiment with new techniques and shows her quilts regularly at national quilt and art shows. Her sense of color and design has won her numerous awards for both quilts and wearable art.

Melinda loves to travel and inspire others with her humorous lecture and fashion show about her artistic development. She also teaches classes in creating Cutting-Garden quilts as well as other projects. She finds it exciting to watch her students grow as they find their own creative styles.

She has designed a line of patterns under the company name Yellow House Designs. The name came about after a much-publicized neighborhood dispute concerning the color of her house. She even made a quilt to commemorate the event. You can see more of her designs or contact her by visiting her Web site at www.melindabula.com.

"Yellow House" was featured in the New York Times.

New and Bestselling Titles from

 That Patchwork Place® — America's Best-Loved Quilt Books®

 Martingale® & COMPANY

America's Best-Loved Craft & Hobby Books®
America's Best-Loved Knitting Books®

APPLIQUÉ
Appliqué Quilt Revival—*NEW!*
Beautiful Blooms
Cutting-Garden Quilts
More Fabulous Flowers—*NEW!*
Sunbonnet Sue and Scottie Too

BABIES AND CHILDREN
Baby Wraps
Lickety-Split Quilts for Little Ones
The Little Box of Baby Quilts
Snuggle-and-Learn Quilts for Kids—*NEW!*
Sweet and Simple Baby Quilts

BEGINNER
Color for the Terrified Quilter
Happy Endings, Revised Edition
Let's Quilt!
Machine Appliqué for the Terrified Quilter
Your First Quilt Book (or it should be!)

GENERAL QUILTMAKING
Adventures in Circles—*NEW!*
Bits and Pieces
Charmed
Cool Girls Quilt
Country-Fresh Quilts—*NEW!*
Creating Your Perfect Quilting Space
Creative Quilt Collection Volume Three
A Dozen Roses
Follow-the-Line Quilting Designs
    Volume Three
Gathered from the Garden—*NEW!*
Points of View
Positively Postcards
Prairie Children and Their Quilts
Quilt Revival
A Quilter's Diary
Quilter's Happy Hour
Simple Seasons
Skinny Quilts and Table Runners
Twice Quilted
Young at Heart Quilts

HOLIDAY AND SEASONAL
Christmas with Artful Offerings
Christmas Quilts from Hopscotch—*NEW!*
Comfort and Joy
Holiday Wrappings—*NEW!*

HOOKED RUGS, NEEDLE FELTING, AND PUNCHNEEDLE
The Americana Collection
Miniature Punchneedle Embroidery
Needle-Felting Magic
Needle Felting with Cotton and Wool
Punchneedle Fun

PAPER PIECING
300 Paper-Pieced Quilt Blocks
A Year of Paper Piecing—*NEW!*
Paper-Pieced Mini Quilts
Show Me How to Paper Piece
Showstopping Quilts to Foundation Piece

PIECING
Copy Cat Quilts
Maple Leaf Quilts
Mosaic Picture Quilts
New Cuts for New Quilts
Nine by Nine
On-Point Quilts—*NEW!*
Ribbon Star Quilts
Rolling Along
Quiltastic Curves
Sew One and You're Done
Square Deal
Sudoku Quilts

QUICK QUILTS
40 Fabulous Quick-Cut Quilts
Instant Bargello—*NEW!*
Quilts on the Double
Sew Fun, So Colorful Quilts
Wonder Blocks

SCRAP QUILTS
Nickel Quilts
Save the Scraps
Simple Strategies for Scrap Quilts
Spotlight on Scraps

CRAFTS
Art from the Heart
The Beader's Handbook
Card Design
Creative Embellishments
Crochet for Beaders
Dolly Mama Beads—*NEW!*
Friendship Bracelets All Grown Up—*NEW!*
It's a Wrap
The Little Box of Beaded Bracelets
    and Earrings
Sculpted Threads
Sew Sentimental

KNITTING & CROCHET
365 Crochet Stitches a Year:
    Perpetual Calendar
365 Knitting Stitches a Year:
    Perpetual Calendar
A to Z of Knitting
Amigurumi World
Cable Confidence
Casual, Elegant Knits—*NEW!*
Chic Knits
Crocheted Pursenalities
First Knits
Gigi Knits...and Purls—*NEW!*
Kitty Knits
The Knitter's Book of Finishing Techniques
Knitting Circles around Socks
Knitting with Gigi
Modern Classics
More Sensational Knitted Socks
Pursenalities
Simple Gifts for Dog Lovers
Skein for Skein—*NEW!*

Our books are available at bookstores and your favorite craft, fabric, and yarn retailers. If you don't see the title you're looking for, visit us at www.martingale-pub.com or contact us at:

1-800-426-3126

International: 1-425-483-3313
Fax: 1-425-486-7596 • Email: info@martingale-pub.com